SCHOLASTIC

Positive Teacher Talk
for Better Classroom Management

Deborah Diffily & Charlotte Sassman

NEW YORK • TORONTO • LONDON • AUCKLAND • SYDNEY
MEXICO CITY • NEW DELHI • HONG KONG • BUENOS AIRES

Teaching *Resources*

Cover design by Maria Lilja
Interior design by Holly Grundon
Photographs by Charlotte Sassman
Illustrations by Maxie Chambliss

ISBN-13 978-0-439-69496-4
ISBN-10 0-439-69496-5
Copyright © 2006 by Deborah Diffily and Charlotte Sassman
All rights reserved.
Printed in the USA.

1 2 3 4 5 6 7 8 9 10   31   12 11 10 09 08 07 06

Contents

CHAPTER 4:

Helping Children Manage Their Behavior 64

CHAPTER 5:

Teaching Language for Specific Situations 84

Foreword

Early childhood educators spend their days talking with and to young children. Some of this conversation is specific to teaching. Some of it describes the activities children are engaged in, helping expand their vocabularies. Some of the language extends children's utterances, thus supporting their general oral language development. Some of it models for children the language of manners and respectful interaction with other people. Some of the chatting with children is simple conversation. Yet, few early childhood educators spend much time thinking about how words may affect those young children.

Teacher talk can positively or negatively affect young children's development. Even when teachers are unaware of what they are doing, their words can encourage children to try new things and support them as they learn to do something new, or their words can discourage children and inadvertently indicate to them that they should not bother trying to learn something. The language that teachers use can either support children's decision making, responsibility, initiative, and teamwork, or it can encourage children to be passive in the classroom, to do only what they are told to do. The language that teachers use can support children's development of autonomy and self-control or it can focus on obedience to school rules.

Chapters in this book discuss how teachers' language affects their young students and offer specific examples of language for different times during the school day that positively support children's development. You can read this book from beginning to end, or you can choose a specific area of teaching in which you want to think more carefully about the language you use. Either way, we encourage you to be reflective about the language you use with and around young children.

Both of us have gone through this process and believe that we are better early childhood educators because we dedicated a considerable amount of time working on improving the language we use with children. We think our students have learned more and developed a greater sense of responsibility as a result.

We wish you luck, and we hope that our thoughts and research will help you in your teaching.

The Importance *of* Teacher Language

Young children use the language they hear spoken around them. Parents and siblings strongly influence young children's vocabularies and the way they learn to put words together to communicate. This influence is obvious when we listen to children's interactions with one another, especially during dramatic-play events. When Patrick is playing the dad and announces, "Don't *make* me come into that bedroom," we pretty much know Patrick has heard that exclamation before. When Donatella cradles a doll in her arms and croons, "It's okay. Everything is going to be okay," we assume that she has seen a parent comforting a crying infant. When Joe proclaims to a classmate, "I'm bigger than you are, so you *have* to do what I say," we guess that he may have heard that particular phrase from an older sibling. Simply put, children pick up the language they hear. The language they use mirrors the language used by people in their lives, yet few people in the lives of young children think about this powerful influence.

Few families specifically plan to teach their children particular phrases or sentences, and when they do, they typically teach phrases associated with the language of manners, such as "please," "thank you," "yes, ma'am," and "no, sir." Few parents teach their children language to help them be successful in group situations such as classes. Children need to know certain language to get along with peers in group situations, get what they want from adults or other children, enter a group of children already engaged in play, or resolve a conflict with a peer. This lack of knowledge about how to interact with other people can be a major stumbling block for children when they become a part of a group at school.

So when children come to school, it becomes the responsibility of teachers to teach all kinds of new vocabulary and different ways of communicating. Children need to learn language that helps them function successfully in groups. We teach them that language. They need to use language that fosters the community-oriented climate we want in our classrooms, so we teach that language as well. We want children to talk with one another in respectful ways, so we teach this too. Teachers of young children purposefully teach all these types of language and support children as they learn the nuances that are appropriate for school settings. Throughout this book, we offer specific strategies for teaching young children the language they need to be successful at school.

Being the Role Model

The first area of language we must consider is our own. The language that we want children to use in our classrooms begins with the language we use and the way we interact with children and other adults in the school. We are our students' role models for school language. Whether we realize it or not, the vocabulary we use, the way we put words together, even our tone of voice are models for our students. Children observe us and listen to what we say all the time, during our purposeful teaching times and during the moments of our most casual interactions. Children learn from what we do throughout the day. Just as Patrick, from the opening vignette, picked up language from his father, incorporating his father's words into his interactions with others, our students inevitably pick up language from us. When we realize what kind of power we have

simply through the language we use, we typically become much more purposeful in modeling appropriate language.

Each teacher has to decide which components of language are most important to model for his or her students. Obviously, every teacher wants to model Standard English. Many children enter our classrooms using a dialect or informal community-influenced language. While we accept and respect children's home languages, at the same time, we need to encourage them to learn and use correct grammar and an increasingly more complex vocabulary. So, as part of working toward this goal, we always model Standard English.

We also want children to speak to one another respectfully, so we model such language as well. We do not want children hurting one another with the language they use, so in our interactions with them, we are careful not to humiliate children or speak to them in condescending ways. We want children to ask one another for things instead of making demands, so we purposefully ask for children's help rather than barking orders at them. We persistently sprinkle our interactions with children with "please," "thank you," and "you're welcome"—phrases of good manners, which, over time, children assimilate into their own interactions with others. In general, we use the same respectful language with children that we would use with adult colleagues.

Developing a Teacher Voice

We all recognize the standard "parent voice" that parents often use to capture their children's attention. How can we, as teachers, get the message across to the children in our classrooms without relying on that kind of "parent voice"? After all, the situation is compounded in the classroom—we deal with dozens of students and organize ever-changing groups of children while still considering each child's individual needs. We want to be assertive with young children by using a voice that commands respect without resorting to a sharp tone. An even-tempered respectful tone is more appropriate for the classroom. Of course, each teacher develops a slightly different teacher voice, depending on his or her personality. But regardless of individual nuances, when we stop and realize the responsibilities we've assumed as major role models for children, it should guide our ideas about developing an appropriate teacher voice.

STORY FROM A FAMILY

I laughingly told my child's teacher that I know everything that goes on in her classroom. She asked me how I knew and I replied that when my daughter gets home, she teaches all of the class's lessons to her dolls. Ashleigh copies Miss Serna's mannerisms and voice inflection perfectly. "She can sound just like you," I told her. "In fact, did you have laryngitis last week?" I asked. When Miss Serna confirmed that she had, I replied, "I thought so. Ashleigh sounded like a croaking frog when she was teaching that day. I asked her about it and she told me Miss Serna had a sore throat." Miss Serna said that she would have to watch her language and mannerisms more closely. I will, too. It is amazing how much children pick up from just watching—at home and at school.

Teachers who value community are especially purposeful in the language they choose to use (DeVries & Zan, 1994). Beyond being careful about the specific words that they use, these teachers generally speak in a quiet voice. They do not bark orders at

children or shout commands over the din of children's voices. Their quiet, even-tempered way of communicating is consistent throughout the day, although there are moments when this quiet voice takes on a different tone. These teachers often speak with passion and enthusiasm when they are launching new topics of study or introducing a new book to the class. Their voices are never quite so captivating as when reading aloud. Their voices ebb and flow as a good story unfolds. There is a measure of surprise and awe when they introduce a new artifact to the class or a hint of mystery when they give clues about an unknown object. In different moments of the day, their teacher voice changes, taking on different nuances. All of these things are purposefully planned to support the classroom community of learners.

Today, television, videos, and other types of mass-media entertainment are particularly engaging for young children. Teachers are forced to compete with actors and cartoons for young children's attention. Thus, teachers often assume voices not unlike actors. These voices are not meant simply to entertain but to capture and maintain the attention of our young students. When children are rambunctious, we drop our voices to just above a whisper. When we are presenting a new topic, the excitement we feel about the subject is palatable. Our tone of voice is driven by what we are trying to accomplish with our students, and all of these voices are part of the teacher voice we try to develop.

STORY FROM A TEACHER

Ms. Maria Cardona, kindergarten

One day, in the middle of math class, I knew that I had to do something to get the children's attention on the idea at hand. All of a sudden, I sat up ramrod straight, put my hands on my knees, and began speaking in a voice reminiscent of an Italian fortune-teller—"The Great Magician does not explain how to do this problem over and over. The Great Magician's powers can help you understand this now." I waved my fingers abracadabra-style and proceeded to explain the concept again, but this time with the children's full attention. It was a corny thing to do, but it got their attention back on the math problem at hand. The Great Magician visits the class intermittently, always unannounced and usually when attention begins to wander.

Using Language That Supports Children's Development

As we know, young children are strongly influenced by the adults around them and the words that those adults use when interacting with them. These words either support the development of young children or hinder it. Sometimes a single statement has a profound effect on a child's development. For example, when a young child is trying to do something independently and a significant adult makes the comment, "Here, let me do that," and takes over the task, the child is less likely to try to do that particular thing independently next time. In extreme cases, children develop a sense of learned helplessness. Taking the opposite stance, when an adult verbalizes encouraging statements, such as, "Look at you. You are trying so hard to zip up your jacket. I am proud of you," these words acknowledge the child's efforts and support the attempt at independence. When we imagine all the physical, social, emotional, and cognitive skills young children need to learn, we are amazed at the influence our words have to support or hinder that development. As we support children in their journey toward independence, we also say things like, "I can see you are about to push in your chair. Thank you for remembering," even when they haven't. This sets up the expectation that they will remember and reinforces the expected behavior.

Sometimes supporting children's development can be as simple as taking a few moments to explain why a particular behavior is important in a situation instead of just demanding that behavior. This is especially true in the area of social development. Encouraging, supportive statements from adults fortify children's emerging development. When a teacher's statement expresses empathy with the drama of a child's life, that is, expresses a belief that the child's feelings are justified, the child senses that the teacher has confidence in him or her. The language that adults use influences a child's development either positively or negatively. Examples of this language are on pages 15–16.

Story From a Family

I remember one moment of my kindergarten year as if it were yesterday—and I am 42 years old. I can close my eyes and see that classroom. I can see other students sitting at their desks working on worksheets, and I can see the teacher sitting in front of me. We had been studying addition for several weeks, and now it was time to "show what we had learned." The students around me had done fine, but I was different. I could not dredge up the answer fast enough for the teacher. When she turned down the last flash card, she looked at me and said, "You are not trying. These facts are easy ones. You are going to have to work harder." I was so embarrassed. She didn't use the word *stupid*, but that is what I heard. If I hadn't been stupid, I would have been able to answer those addition equations. From that day on, I've had a hard time with math. I've always wondered if I would have had problems with math if my teacher had said something more supportive, like, "I know you can do this. We'll work on it together." Sometimes one comment from a teacher can affect you for life.

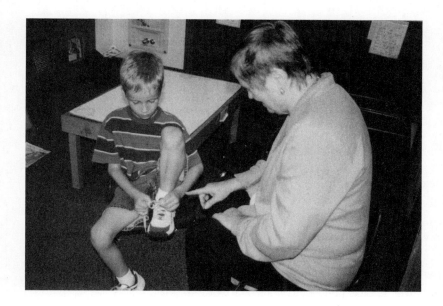

Positive
TEACHER TALK

Hindering vs. Supporting Phrases

Consider how the following statements may hinder or support a young child's development:

"If you can't share, then I'm taking it away from you."
— vs. —
"I know it is hard to share your toys, but when Jake is finished with the truck, I am sure he will let you have a turn."

· ·

"Don't snatch things!"
— vs. —
"He was using that marker. If you want to use it, you need to ask politely. Try saying, 'May I please use that marker when you are finished?'"

· ·

"Do not hit!"
— vs. —
"I know he hit you first, but people are not for hitting. When you get angry, here are some things you can do, like (offer two options), but I cannot let anyone in this room hit anyone else."

Continued next page

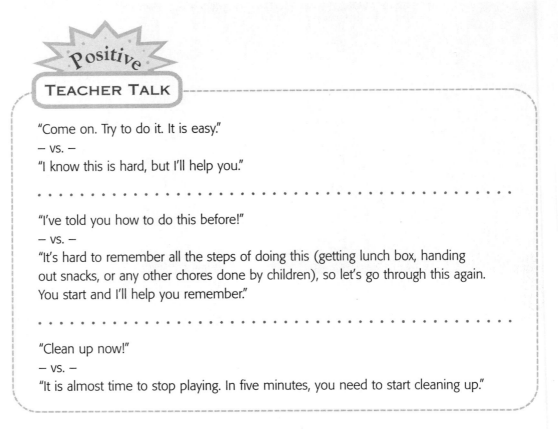

"Come on. Try to do it. It is easy."
— vs. —
"I know this is hard, but I'll help you."

. . . .

"I've told you how to do this before!"
— vs. —
"It's hard to remember all the steps of doing this (getting lunch box, handing out snacks, or any other chores done by children), so let's go through this again. You start and I'll help you remember."

. . . .

"Clean up now!"
— vs. —
"It is almost time to stop playing. In five minutes, you need to start cleaning up."

Using Language That Guides Children

Just as adults' language can support or hinder a child's development, it can also guide young children into appropriate behaviors. Most early childhood educators want children to become autonomous. We want children to act in appropriate ways because that is the right thing to do. So, rather than demand certain behaviors, teachers are more likely to guide children into more appropriate choices for their behavior.

One way to do this is by limiting the number of choices a child has in a particular situation. When Reginald grabs the science hand lens instead of waiting his turn, the teacher says, "Reginald, you may wait until Dameon is finished or you may get another lens from our supply. You may not grab a tool that someone is using." Likewise, when Taramoni runs across the room during transition time, the teacher says, "Taramoni, in this room you either walk or you are the last to move. Which behavior do you choose?" In both examples, the teacher may have given other choices. Dameon could have been removed from the group, made to miss recess, etc. Taramoni could have been made to return to her beginning spot and walk again. However, these solutions simply punish the child instead of guiding a change in the child's behavior. It is important to remember that in early childhood classes children do not naturally relate punishment with the offending actions. Redirection and guidance are more often the appropriate ways to address misbehavior.

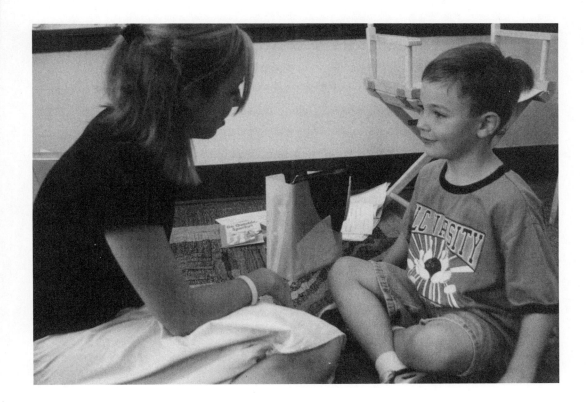

TEACHER TALK

Guiding Children Into More Appropriate Behaviors

★ "What are we supposed to be doing right now?"

★ "Is _____ appropriate behavior?"

★ "Are you being self-controlled? What would self-control look like (in this situation)?"

★ "What do we do in our class when that happens?"

★ "In our class meeting, we decided to do _____. Please respect the class's decision."

★ "Tell me two things that you might do instead of _____. Are those respectful ways to solve the problem? Which do you choose?"

★ "In our class, we _____."

Teaching Respectful Language

Using respectful language—teachers to children, children to children, and children to teachers—is central to developing a community of learners (Bickart, Jablon & Dodge, 1999). In addition to modeling appropriate language and using language that supports development and guides children, we use a number of teaching strategies so that children learn appropriate language for school.

First, we teach children the language of a community. This teaching often occurs in the context of a class meeting or while we work with pairs or small groups of children who are having a particular problem. Also, we frequently use children's literature to focus attention on typical interpersonal problems and to pose possible alternatives for solving those problems. We plan opportunities for children to practice using respectful language in different contexts. And, of course, we give children reminders as often as they need them.

We begin teaching respectful language from the first moment we begin interacting with a child. On the first day of school, when we greet children, we begin modeling respectful language. A kind, soft voice supports children as they begin their first day of school. A genuine welcome puts families at ease as they leave their children in our care. A teacher who is trying to establish a caring, supportive atmosphere welcomes children to the classroom in the morning. These words of welcome begin each day with respectful language and model ways in which children can interact with one another.

Teachers also teach specific words, phrases, and sentences that are respectful ways to communicate and also support a sense of community (Charney, 1992). Even before the school year begins, think about examples of respectful language that children need to learn. These phrases can be taught in class meetings or simply suggested when children use language that is not respectful. For example, if one child demands, "Give me that blue crayon," you might respond with, "Instead of saying, 'Give me that crayon,' please ask for it. Say, 'Would you please hand me a blue crayon?'" If a child screams, "Get out of my way. It's my turn to paint," you might say, "That is not very respectful. Please ask for a turn. Say, 'When you finish painting, I would like to be next.'" Children may not begin using your suggested language immediately or they may use it in a rote, superficial way. However, over time, they internalize and begin using the language that is respectful and appropriate for the classroom.

Summary

Because young children's language is so influenced by those around them, be careful to act as appropriate role models for your young students. Find your own "teacher voice," one that captures and maintains the attention of your students. Use language that supports children's development and guides them into appropriate behaviors. In addition to modeling respectful language, specifically teach respectful words, phrases, and sentences.

Welcoming Children

I t does not matter how many years we've taught, the first day of school is always a bit unnerving. Although we've set up the classroom, planned age-appropriate lessons and other learning experiences, and are ready—at least logistically—for a new group of children, we do not sleep very much the night before the first day of school. Images of children run through our minds. Potential problems play out among all those images.

As we prepare to begin a new school year, we downplay our own nervous feelings and concentrate on the feelings of the young children who enter our classroom. Transitions are not easy for young children, and beginning a new school year is a major transition. We think through all the things that we have learned from experience that help put young children at ease: a cheerful-looking room; lots of smiles; a soft, reassuring voice; upbeat songs; and engaging read alouds. We run through the schedule for the day that we have planned. It alternates between active and passive activities and provides many activities in which children begin to work together and get to know one another. We even review what we are going to wear, what to say to individuals and to the group, and when during the day to say it. In all of our plans for the first day of school, we want to put children at ease, making them feel comfortable and welcome in our classrooms.

Greeting Each Child

First impressions are important—especially for young children. For each child in your classroom, your first smile and your first words can set the tone for the entire school year. The words need to be specific to each child and delivered in a warm, welcoming manner.

Some of the welcoming words you might use are listed below:

Welcoming Words

★ "Hello, I am glad that you are here today."

★ "I am so happy you are in our class."

★ "I am so glad to meet you."

★ "I've got a special book about the first day of school I want to read to you right after you spend some time playing with the play dough at that table right over there."

★ "This is our classroom. What things do you see that you like?"

★ "Looks like you dressed very carefully for today."

★ "You have a red backpack and I have a red shirt. We must both like red."

★ "You have the nicest smile!"

★ "You look ready to start school. What do you want to learn this year?"

★ "Is this your family? How lucky you are that your little brother came with you!"

These first words to each student also need to convey the message that the child's opinions and contributions are valued in this classroom. You can inquire about a child's expectations for the year; for example, "What do you want to learn this year?" or "Have you been thinking about what you want to have for a class pet?" Extending the child's response to indicate that other members of the community have a voice as well reinforces the idea that this classroom is a place where everyone's ideas are considered.

STORY FROM A CHILD

Ashley, beginning of 1st grade

I was scared to go in the room on the first day of school. Mommy said, "It's okay. This is your first-grade room. Go in." But I didn't want to. Then Ms. Jonas came out in the hall and held my hand. She said, "I'm so glad you are here today. Come on in." She says that to me every day. I like Ms. Jonas.

STORY FROM A TEACHER

Ms. Charlotte Sassman, 1st grade

When I am planning the room arrangement, I always include a few extra chairs in a few different areas of the room. That way, when I want to get on a child's level, all I have to do is grab a child-sized chair from the nearby center and we can talk on the same level.

Another thing that works for me is to make some of the tables shorter. Then I can sit on the tabletop and be on the same level as the child. Also, some situations or discussions seem to go better if the child can sit in a chair and I can sit on the floor. Sometimes just allowing the child to be "taller" than me settles them down and reinforces that idea that everyone's opinion is valued and listened to.

To make the tables shorter, I adjust the legs a bit lower and do away with the chairs. Children just sit on the floor when they work at this table. Another good thing about this is that lowering the tables and eliminating the chairs remove more distractions from the room. After all, when there are no chairs no one has to be reminded to "keep the chair's legs on the floor" or "push your chair in when you leave."

Heather, beginning of kindergarten

I was scared on my first day. I was holding Mommy's hand. Then Mommy showed me my new teacher. She was sitting in a chair talking to Jason. Mommy pushed me to my teacher and Mrs. Grissom reached out and held my hand. That made me feel better. I could hold her hand just like Mommy's. Then she said she was really glad that I was in her class. I was still a little nervous, but she wanted me in her class, so I figured it would be an okay day.

For example, after you ask a child, "What do you want to learn this year?" you might encourage him or her to begin (or add to) a list of "Things We Want to Learn" posted near the front of the room. Then, at group time, the entire class can review the list, add to it, prioritize the items, and decide on which one (or ones) to address first.

Another simple way to reinforce this partnership between you and the child is to bend over or crouch down so that you are speaking from the same level as the child. Positioning yourself so that you are eye-to-eye with the child, rather than looking down at the child from a standing position, communicates that the child is important to you. If constant bending over is a problem for you, put a low chair near the door and greet children from there.

Stage-managing the initial greeting and other one-on-one interactions with children goes a long way toward establishing the atmosphere you want in your classroom. There are other things you can do to foster a good relationship with each child as well.

ESTABLISHING RELATIONSHIPS

Teachers need to work to establish a relationship with each student in the class, but relationship building does not end there. Teachers also need to think about the adults in the lives of their students. When you consider your feelings before the first day of school and realize how apprehensive you are (and remember, you are the one in control of planning the activities and interactions), imagine the level of apprehension the children's families are feeling. They are entrusting their child to your care and do not really know anything about you. They would not arrange for child care without recommendation, so remember, they are seeking information about you as well. Make sure they get accurate information (rather than gossip from a neighbor who "once heard that Miss So-and-So did thus-and-such"). Sending letters to children before school starts, telephoning families, arranging for a get-acquainted meeting, or simply being available in the classroom before the first day of school are strategies to use to establish relationships between you and the children in your class.

SENDING LETTERS HOME BEFORE SCHOOL STARTS

The eternal question of "who will be my new teacher?" tops every child's list as he or she thinks about school before the year begins. Many of them have preconceived notions about who the "best" teacher is and who they "want" for their teacher. Older siblings have a great deal of influence on this, as do neighbors and friends. One way to actively introduce yourself is to send each child and family a letter of introduction. This can be a simple postcard welcoming the child to the classroom or a more detailed letter that includes biographical information about you, your expectations for the year as well as the first day, supplies the children need to bring, etc. The method you choose depends on the circumstances involved. Consider the approaches used by these two teachers:

Lena, a first-year teacher, was overwhelmed by all the things she had to do to get ready for the beginning of school. She decided that she only had time to jot a quick postcard to the children in her class. She wanted them to be personalized so she handwrote a quick greeting to each one. (Hello! I am glad you are in my class. I'll see you on Tuesday. From, Miss Pugliano)

Another first-year teacher, Cynthia, was feeling the same pressure. Cynthia decided to create a blanket letter to her class on the computer and mail copies to each family. Cynthia wrote about herself—her background, schooling, and family—and briefly outlined some goals for the school year.

Both took about the same length of time, but the note and the letter had different impacts. Cynthia's families were reassured. Some of their questions were answered. They had the feeling that they knew a little bit about the new teacher and got the impression that she was a warm, open person. Cynthia's families made a personal connection with her—perhaps it was through her comments about her background or her favorite activities, but the important thing was that the families felt a personal connection. Though Lena's families felt the note mailed to their children was a nice touch, they did not feel that they had learned anything about her.

When writing a before-school-starts letter, think about what families may want to know about you and your class. You might include some of these things:

- ★ A general welcoming statement

- ★ A brief description of the classroom—something that the child or parents might look for on that first day

- ★ Some of the learning goals for the year

★ Brief descriptions of some of the learning experiences planned for the first week (or month) of the school year

★ Some personal information, e.g., educational background, teaching experience, family members, hobbies, etc.

★ Questions you would like the family to answer in a letter written back to you, e.g., What are some things about your child that would be important for me to know? When your child is upset, what calms him or her? What are some of your child's interests? What are some of your family's favorite activities?

If you are a first-year teacher or starting in a new situation, families may naturally feel some apprehension about you. This letter is an opportunity to address their fears or concerns and direct their apprehensions in a positive manner.

Sample Before-the-School-Year-Begins Letter

Dear Families:

School begins in two weeks. I am looking forward to meeting each one of you and working together to make this a very special year for your children. Before we meet, I would like to share a few things about me, and I hope that in return you will share some things about you, your child, and your family.

I became a kindergarten teacher when I was in my 30s. This is my 17th year of teaching in pre-kindergarten, kindergarten, or first-grade classes. I find this age group simply fascinating.

I believe that young children learn best when they are active and when they make many decisions about their learning. On the first day of school, you will notice that our classroom is organized by learning centers. Most of our day will be spent working in these centers: art, blocks, dramatic play, listening, math, music, reading, sand and water, science, and writing. The room may seem a little bare. That is by design. I want the children to feel a sense of ownership of the classroom, so we will create bulletin boards, classroom labels, and work displays together.

I would like to know about your family. Please take a few minutes in the next few days and write whatever you think would help me get to know your child and your family. You may want to consider answering these questions: What is your child like? What upsets your child, and what calms him or her? What are some of your child's interests? What do you like to do as a family?

I am looking forward to reading your letters and to meeting all of you. I think this will be a great year as we work together.

Sincerely,

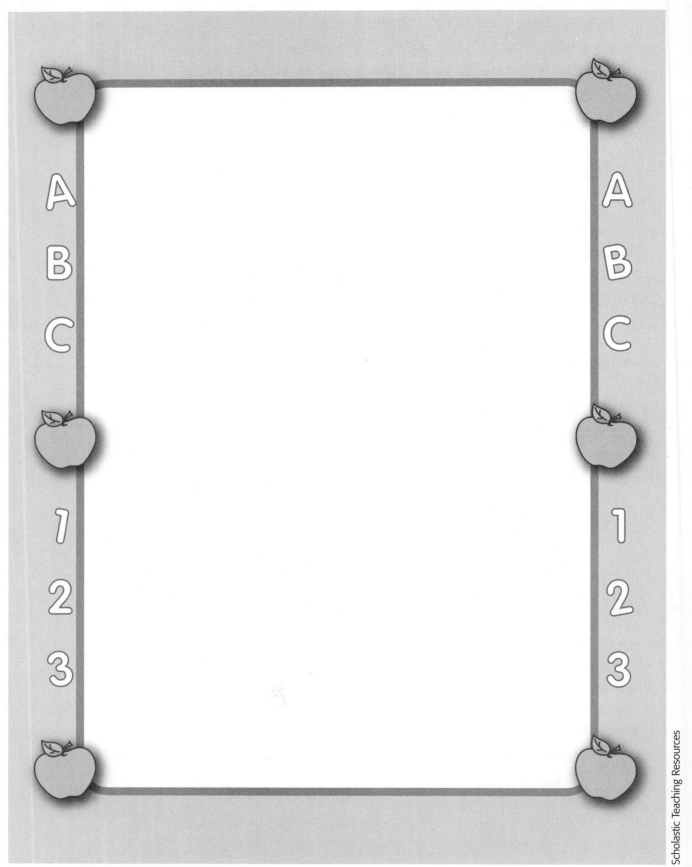

Stationery for Family Letters

TELEPHONING STUDENTS

Another personal way to reach out to families is to make telephone calls. Plan three or four points to make during the call. It is a good idea to speak to the parent first. That way, you can introduce yourself and give the parent a glimpse of classroom life and ask a couple of questions about the child before speaking to him or her. Remember that the child may be shy or hesitant about answering questions. Asking open-ended questions or soliciting opinions tends to promote more conversation.

Before calling a family, be sure to get your administrator's support. In some situations, the school principal may know things about a family that would be good for you to know before you call. Some teachers prefer that families of their students do not have their home telephone numbers, so they make all their phone calls from school. Also, be sure to plan what to do if the family does not answer and you get an answering machine. You may want your message to give the family a bit of the information you wanted to share or to simply tell them that you will call back. A sample response for an answering machine follows:

Possible Answering Machine Message

"Hi, this is Miss Tarvin from Glencrest Elementary School. I wanted to talk to the family, especially to Joanna who will be a student in my first-grade class. Joanna, start thinking of the kinds of things you want to learn about this year. Bring some ideas to share with the others on the first day of school. I've been moving the furniture around in our classroom and getting all the books out. I really like to read books to children and I hope you like that, too. I'll be looking for you on Monday when school starts. Come to room 12 at 8:30 and I'll be waiting for you. Good-bye."

GET-ACQUAINTED DINNER

Some schools have a "back-to-school" dinner or picnic. It is usually held on the school grounds or in the cafeteria. The idea of having an informal, come-and-go opportunity to eat and talk makes the situation less intimidating for the families and the teacher. Families get an opportunity to talk individually with you, and you get to observe how families interact with one another. This is a good time to take photographs of each child and his or her family as well. You can develop these photographs and create a bulletin board illustrating "Our Families." The photographs can also be posted inside the children's lockers, reminding the children of their families' support.

STORY FROM A TEACHER

Ms. Delores Echols, kindergarten

When I first came to my new school I was nervous about meeting all the families. I knew this was a school that valued family participation and I was not used to that. Even though I had taught for seven years, I was unsure of what to say. So I planned a simple interactive treasure hunt for the kids to do. It was a hit! This gave the children something to do while I visited with their families and got a quick look at who could follow directions, cooperate, etc. I also took pictures of each family to use on a bulletin board. But even better than getting a good bulletin board out of those photographs, they allowed me to put names and faces together faster than ever. That get-together was on Friday, and by the start of school on Monday I knew which child went with which adult. That was a big plus for me!

When dinner is served in the school's cafeteria and teachers are in their classrooms to meet the families, families can come to the classroom, visit with the teacher one on one, and then move to the cafeteria to eat. If a family thinks of other questions or comments, they can return to the classroom after eating. This helps control the amount of time that each family spends with the teacher. If one family tries to dominate your time, you might say, "I know you want to move to the cafeteria to eat and I need to talk to Richard's family. Come back when you finish eating."

Providing name tags for everyone (siblings and other family members) provides a bit of an icebreaker as families come into the room. They may be unsure of what to do, so having this small task can give them a minute to get acclimated to the room. We usually put tags and pens near the door with a small sign indicating that they are to complete a name tag. Then if you get busy as several families arrive, no one feels left out. After a couple of families are present, you might ask their children (or them) to act as the welcoming committee for other families.

Getting conversations started can be difficult. You want to talk to each family, but you also want families to talk to one another. If you can introduce the families to one another with a comment about something they have in common, it helps get them talking. You need to move from family to family so everyone gets an opportunity to talk with you.

Talking to children during this time can be a bit tricky, too. The class has not yet met and guidelines for using the things in the room have not been discussed. Often children are not being closely supervised as their parents talk to other families, and they look at this as "free play" time. If you think this may happen, put away particularly messy classroom materials (such as play dough or paint) or those with lots of pieces (such as puzzles or Legos®) until you and the children have time to learn to use them. It is helpful to direct children to activities that are okay for them to use. For example, say, "I put all

---

STORY FROM A FAMILY

I did not know anyone but my next-door neighbor who went to my child's new school. The school scheduled a "Meet and Greet" dinner on the Friday night before school started. That was a great stress-reliever for me. I got to know the teacher and had a chance to really talk with just her, instead of hearing her talk in a group meeting. Also, I met some other single moms. We ended up forming a dinner group that meets once a month and shares child-care arrangements. Even though I was apprehensive about going, I'm so glad I did. It was good for my child and maybe even better for me.

the cardboard blocks out near the back of the room if you like to build," or "Here are some dominos to play with." Some other helpful phrases are listed below:

INFORMALLY MEETING BEFORE SCHOOL STARTS

Most school districts incorporate at least one day of preparation time for teachers to organize their classrooms. If you are willing to share your preparation time, this can be an opportunity to invite children to come to the classroom informally and meet you. Sometimes the office staff can inform families of this opportunity as children enroll, or a notice can be mailed to families. This option may not be convenient for all the families in your class because not everyone can arrange their schedule to come to school during the workday. You may want to consider extending the time beyond the regular school day so working parents can participate as well.

The same kinds of conversations go on in this situation as at the back-to-school dinner, except that you will probably have a bit more time to spend with each family. Still, connecting the families with one another, observing their interactions, and greeting children should be your main focus.

COMMUNICATING WITH FAMILIES

The adults who bring children to their classrooms on the first day of school also need some reassurance from the teacher. Adults are a secondary audience on this day. We always talk to the child first. It is most important that their child feels comfortable with us and in the classroom. We try to make what we say to the child also communicate with his or her families. For example, after an initial greeting to the child, we might say, "I've put play dough on each of the tables in our room. Take your mom into the room and find your favorite color of play dough. Then you and your mom can make something with the play dough. Do you think you want to make some round balls or flat pancakes or long, skinny snakes or something else? I'll bet you and your mom can make something very interesting. The tables are right over there. I'll let you know when it is time to clean up and come to the group area."

These comments, directed to the child, also communicate to the parents. They let parents know it is okay to go into the classroom and engage in an activity with their child. They know that they are not expected to leave immediately. They also know what kind of activity they should lead their child into and what happens next. This way, as they talk with their child, they can prepare him or her for the time that they will leave, as well.

As the official school day draws near, we walk around the classroom giving notice that it will soon be time for the accompanying adults to leave. We say something like, "In about three minutes, gather with me on the carpet. When I say clean up, roll your play dough into a ball and put it in the plastic bag." After visiting all the tables, we say, in a slightly louder voice, "Thank you so much for listening. Please roll your play dough into a ball now and put it in the plastic bag. Leave the bag on the table and join me in the group." We go around the room, helping individual children as needed, and then head for the group area.

At this time, most of the accompanying adults will leave the classroom. We begin to read a book to the children, sing a song, or act out a chant. The children are engaged in an activity, and the adults can leave, feeling like their children are in a good place. If the adults do not leave, we say, "Boys and girls, it is time for the grown-ups to go to work or take care of their business. We are ready to start our day and they need to start their day. So wave good-bye to them and we will see them this afternoon in the front, by the big tree." We wave and continue immediately with the planned activity, focusing on the children and ignoring the adults as they leave. This sends a message to children that we are going to listen and pay attention to them. It also tells the adults that our focus is with their children, and we are there to help their children adjust to the day.

Of course, there is often the crying child or the one who clings to the adult. In this case, we offer the child a bit more time for the separation, saying, "Juan, would you like for your mom to join us in the group? She can sit with us for a short time and then we have our work to do." This gives the child and adult one more chance at making the separation successful. Asking that child to move closer (while the adult stays in the background) or to take part in a role-play also helps ease the separation. If these strategies do not work, we continue to be reassuring, but encourage the adult to leave, stressing to the child that the adult will return to pick him or her up in the afternoon. Then we move the child near us, possibly sitting on the floor so he or she can be right beside us. After the adult leaves, the child usually stops crying and settles down. At this point, we compliment the way the child handled the situation. We might say, "You were so brave this morning when your aunt left. I know it was hard to say good-bye but she will be back this afternoon to get you. It is my job to take care of you while you are at school and that's just what I will do. Can I count on you for help?"

Invariably there is the child who experiences much difficulty with separating from the adult. Sometimes the adult must be urged to leave, even as the child cries or screams. Sometimes this is upsetting to the other children, so we speak directly to them about the child's disruptive behavior. By saying, "Boys and girls, you are being such nice friends to Jarrett. He is having a hard time saying good-bye to his dad. I know you know

how he is feeling. Could you be especially friendly to him so he'll feel like he has lots of friends and is not alone at school?" you are reinforcing to the crying child as well as to the other children that you take care of everyone and that the feelings of everyone in the class are important.

Talking With the Whole Class

After those first words of greeting, the next time a teacher talks to children is usually as a whole group. Those first few words are important—the words themselves, the tone of voice, and the nonverbal communication as well.

You need to decide how you are going to refer to the whole group of students. Both of us use different terms. Charlotte refers to her students as "friends" or "learners." Deborah uses "ladies and gentlemen," "friends," or "guys," depending on the reason she's addressing them as a group. There is not one term that works best, but you do need to think about what word or words you use and what those words may communicate to your students.

These first words to the whole class need to be welcoming and reassuring. We always tell our new students how happy we are for them to be in our classes, that we've thought about them all summer and planned a lot of exciting things for us to do. This initial conversation with the class usually needs to be brief. The language you choose needs to communicate that this class is a safe, warm place to be and that you are excited about all the things that you will do together. Then we usually turn to the class's first read aloud.

A Classroom Conversation

A First Whole-Group Conversation on the First Day of School

Mrs. Marlin: Good morning, friends. I am so glad that you are all in our class this year. I've talked with each one of you, and I can honestly say that this is a wonderful group of first-grade students. It will take a few days, but during this first week of school, you will have time to get to know one another. You will make friends in this class, and all together, we are going to have a great year.

I want to start this morning by having us all think about good teachers. I want to be a good teacher for each one of you, so I want you to think for a minute about what good teachers do. I want you to say what you think, but only one at a time, so I can write down your thoughts. Watch as I write: "What Good Teachers Do." [Teacher writes this title on the top line of a chart tablet, then transcribes children's comments in the following conversation.]

Jorge: Are nice.

Mrs. Marlin: Okay, good teachers are nice. What else?

Dana: Good teachers let you go outside for a long recess.

Mrs. Marlin: Okay, recess is important to you, eh? I like recess, too. Who else has an idea about what good teachers do?

Travis: Let you paint on the easel and make things with clay.

Mrs. Marlin: Ooh, you like to create pieces of artwork and think that good teachers provide those things that you need to be creative. Is it okay if I write down "encourages creativity"? Okay, I'll write that. Who else has an idea?

Tom:	Teachers tell you true facts.
Mrs. Marlin:	Tom, I am glad you think good teachers share interesting facts. I know a lot of interesting facts I can't wait to share with this class. In fact, I'll start that this afternoon. Who else?
Janet:	Good teachers read lots of stories.
Mrs. Marlin:	That is another thing I love to do, read lots and lots of stories to my class. Who else besides Janet thinks that good teachers read lots of stories? Show me a thumbs-up if you agree with Janet. *[Notes how many children give the thumbs-up sign.]* Great. Now, I'm ready to write down another idea about good teachers.
Paige:	Good teachers help kids.
Mrs. Marlin:	Oh, yes. I think that that is an important part of a teacher's job, helping children learn. *[Pauses, waiting for other children to contribute.]* Okay, maybe some of you need some more time to think about what good teachers do. We will continue this conversation and this list tomorrow. But there is one more thing I want to say about this list.

I am not the only teacher in this room. Some people think that I am the teacher and you are the learners, but I really don't see us in that way. I think of myself as a learner, like you guys. I am always learning new things. And I don't see you guys as just learners. You already know many things that you can teach to other people. So I see us all as teachers and learners.

Let's go back over what we've already written down. *[Reads list aloud, pointing to words while reading.]* See, many of these things are things that you can do. You can be nice to classmates, right? You can tell true facts to one another, and you can read stories to one another, and you can help other students, right? I want you to remember, everyone in this room is a teacher and everyone in this room is a learner. Now, it's time for us to _____.

Literature LINKS

Great First-Day-of-School Books

There are a number of books that are good to use as a springboard for discussions about different aspects of life at school. Here are a few:

Clifford's First School Day by Norman Bridwell (Scholastic, 1999)
As a small puppy, Clifford goes to school with Emily Elizabeth and gets into mischievous trouble during finger-painting, cookie-baking, and snack times.

. . . .

Look Out Kindergarten, Here I Come! by Nancy L. Carlson (Puffin, 2001)
Henry is not so sure he's ready for kindergarten. But before long he discovers that the only thing he's not ready for is how much fun he's going to have at school.

. . . .

First Day Jitters by Julie Danneberg (Charlesbridge, 2000)
Sarah Jane is worried about going to a new school. She refuses to get out of bed because she keeps imagining all the bad things that can happen. The surprise twist at the end—that Sarah Jane is the teacher—delights children.

. . . .

Little Miss Spider at Sunnypatch School by David Kirk (Scholastic, 2000)
Continuing the familiar series, on her first day at school, Little Miss Spider worries that she cannot do what the others can, but she learns that she has her own special quality.

. . . .

First Day, Hooray! by Nancy Poydar (Holiday House, 2000)
Children are not the only ones who start the first day of school. This book addresses kids' beginning-of-school worries while presenting the adults' point of view as well.

. . . .

Twelve Days of Kindergarten: A Counting Book by Deborah Lee Rose
(Harry N. Abrams, 2003)
Patterned after the familiar carol "The Twelve Days of Christmas," this book offers a welcome introduction to school. By the twelfth day the children have discovered that they love school. The book features cardinal and ordinal numbers.

Continued next page

David Goes to School by David Shannon (Scholastic, 1999)
David's activities in school include chewing gum, talking out of turn, and engaging in a food fight, causing his teacher to say over and over, "No, David!" This book offers plenty of opportunities to discuss beginning-of-school behavior.

. . . .

Miss Bindergarten Gets Ready for Kindergarten by Joseph Slate (Puffin, 2001)
This delightful, rhyming text introduces the letters of the alphabet, as Miss Bindergarten and her students prepare for the start of school.

. . . .

Mouse's First Day of School by Lauren Thompson (Simon & Schuster, 2003)
When he goes to school, Mouse finds a world of new objects and new friends.

. . . .

My Teacher Sleeps in School by Leatie Weiss (Puffin, 1985)
Because Mrs. Marsh is always in her classroom before the students arrive and always stays after they leave, Mollie becomes convinced that her teacher has no home other than the school. So the children in Mrs. Marsh's class search for clues to prove their teacher sleeps in school.

. . . .

The Night Before Kindergarten by Natasha Wing (Grosset & Dunlap, 2001)
When a group of children prepares for and experiences the first day of kindergarten, it is the parents who are the ones having trouble adjusting.

Introducing Children to One Another

Another task teachers have on this all-important first day (or week) of school is introducing children to one another and helping them begin to feel like part of a special group of children. Most young children come into their classrooms as strangers to one another. For some children, making new friends is very natural. They seem to reach out to other children automatically. For others, being in a room full of strangers is difficult. They sit back and watch other children. They do not know what to do to engage peers. It is our job to help children get to know one another. The words we use not only make children feel at ease but also facilitate their becoming familiar with one another.

Often one of the first activities of the day during the first week or two of the school year relates to children's names. A favorite whole-group game involves orally stating names and a "favorite" thing. Sit with children in a large circle so all participants can see each person's face. Start the game by stating your name and telling a "favorite." We often start the game with favorite foods, colors, sports, books, cartoons, etc. Invite children to respond in the same manner. During the responses, continuously repeat the child's name and relate children with common interests together. You might say, "Wow! Lawrence and Lolli both like pizza. And their names start with /l/. They have two things in common."

One of the simplest things we can do that first day of school is to use children's names continually during group meetings and small-group activities. The more we refer to children by their names, the quicker they will learn one another's names. This is the first step to becoming friends. Simply saying, "Ming, join Jonathon on the bench to read" helps both Ming and Jonathon learn each other's names and establish the beginnings of a friendship. We purposefully use children's names as often as possible during the first few weeks of school to support them in this process.

Young children enjoy singing games with their names. Sung to the tune of "Bingo," this song gets children involved and moving as well. Begin by singing: "There was a class that had a girl (boy) / And _____ was her name-o / Jump, jump, _____ / Jump, jump, _____ / Jump, jump, _____ / We're so glad you came today." Invite children to join in as they become familiar with the tune. You can vary the movement to fit the situation—sit, clap, walk, tap, etc.

Another game for kindergartners involves matching children's names with name cards in a pocket chart. We prepare two sets of different-colored name cards, cutting sentence strips into name-sized cards. We put the cards on the floor in the middle of the group area and gather children in a large circle. Each child gets his or her own name card and then children move to face the pocket chart. Then we say, "If your name is Roger, come put your card on top of the pink card that says 'Roger.'" During the first few times you play, give clear, precise directions that repeatedly use the names. As children become more familiar with one another's names, give clues that relate to other things about the child. For example, "If you have one kitten as a pet and you like to play jump rope, come put your card on top of your pink card." First- and second-grade children enjoy counting the number of letters in their names and finding another child with a matching number of letters. As children begin to match their names, be sure to repeat the names and connect children with their names. All of these games reinforce children's names and help them get to know one another.

Introducing Daily Activities

Young children find comfort in the predictable nature of the day's activities. When they know their morning begins by making a choice from the ABC center, followed by group time, during which the teacher first reads a story and then conducts a lesson, followed by independent center work, they feel safe, confident, and comfortable (Bickart et al., 1999).

Positive
TEACHER TALK

Phrases to Describe Different Activities

Say . . .	. . . to Indicate . . .
★ "Be sure you have enough room for your space bubble."	children should sit close to one another but not touching one another.
★ "Come to the carpet (group area, etc.)."	a particular area of the room.
★ "When we go to the hall, remember to wait at our stopping place."	the area for waiting or lining up.
★ "Go to your places."	the area of the room where children should sit for a particular activity.

Teachers who understand this need present the daily activities in a predictable way each day. Although the first day of school can require some adaptations to the usual schedule, sticking to the basics of the everyday schedule sets the tone for the rest of the year. It is important to schedule the activities on the first day in the same order as they will occur in the regular schedule. For example, if the daily schedule calls for reading and then writing, follow that schedule on the first day. You may have to abbreviate (or extend) some of the activities but keep them in the same order.

The language used to describe different activities on the first day of school also stays with children throughout the year, so it is important to think through the procedures and terminology for that first day. The way you first describe the features of the classroom becomes the way children think of them all year long. See the box on page 39 for examples.

Establishing Routines

Just as you introduce activities on the first day of school that become a part of children's daily schedule, you also begin teaching children some of the routines that guide the class. When routines are in place, the class operates much more smoothly. We explicitly teach certain routines and have children practice them. On the first day of school, we limit the number of routines we teach to two or three so children do not feel overwhelmed. Some of our first-day routines include listening to other people, stopping an activity and looking at the teacher, and sitting in the group area. Other typical routines for early childhood classes include going to the bathroom, working in a small group, putting work where it belongs, cleaning up, and getting ready to go home.

Just as teachers need to be specific about what they expect from children during daily activities, they need to think about the language they use to describe routines. The description needs to be succinct but also include all the steps of the routine. For example, when a teacher tells the class to "come to the meeting area" or "get ready to go home," it may mean ten different things to ten different children. But when a teacher explains exactly what these routines look like and supports children's learning by practicing the routine several times, they are likely to remember what to do. The descriptive words need to be the same, repeated and practiced day after day, until all children learn each routine. See the box on page 41 for specific words to describe a particular routine.

Teaching the Coming-to-Group-Meeting Routine

"Listen very carefully. Some of you put the play dough right into the container when I asked you to put it away. You walked right to the meeting area when I said, 'Come, sit beside me on the floor.' But some of you did not come right away. Some of you kept playing with the play dough until I walked to your table and asked you to put it in the container a second time. Some of you kept talking and did not come to the meeting area until I asked you to a third time. In this class, we come to the meeting area the first time we are asked. Let's try that again. Please walk back to where you were working with the play dough. Pretend you are playing play dough and listen very carefully. When I say, 'Put the play dough away and come to the meeting area,' that's what I want you to do. Can we try that?"

For every routine you introduce to your students your explanation needs to be just as specific as the example of coming-to-group-meeting routine. In some cases, you may want to write out the words you use to describe a routine to your class. This helps you be consistent. Another way to remind children of the expected behavior is to draw simple pictures to illustrate the sequence of the routine. A simple visual reminder with numbered steps clearly communicates your expectations to the class.

There are other parts of the first day of school when teacher language is very important, such as teaching children to work together (discussed in chapter 3) and teaching behavioral expectations (discussed in chapter 4).

Summary

Individually greeting each child on the first day of school is a small gesture that helps communicate that the classroom is a warm, safe place to be. That first interaction between you and a child establishes the basis for a relationship that grows throughout the school year. During the first day, introduce children to one another, to activities, and to routines.

Setting the Tone for the Year

The first few days—and weeks—of school set the tone for the entire year. Most young children quickly learn the expectations of the teacher and school, and then they begin to practice their responses to those expectations. Obviously, different children bring different life experiences to the classroom. It becomes your responsibility to pull this diverse group together, to teach not only the curriculum but also the language that leads to appropriate decision making, friendship making, collaboration, and responsibility.

Learning About Each Child

Knowing each child as an individual is integral to effective teaching. It seems impossible as you start the school year to know each one of the twenty-five or so children in your class. Add his or her family members and mix in a few friends—soon you have almost a hundred new people. The thought of getting to know this many people can be daunting; however, by breaking it down into manageable parts, you can start the process.

Many teachers start gathering information about each child by looking at the information cards completed by the families. When a family enrolls a child in school, they provide basic information about their child and themselves. You can gain other information by reading between the lines. For example, if the mother and father have

---

STORY FROM A TEACHER

Ms. Katherine Sheffield, kindergarten

Today, while we were singing and dancing in music class, Jamel commented that all of his big brothers dance. I said, "Jamel, you don't have big brothers." He replied, "Yes, I do—four of them." I questioned him about his brothers, and he had answers to all my questions. But there were no brothers listed on his family information card. That afternoon, I asked Jamel's mother about the four big brothers. They did indeed exist. They were half brothers from his father's first marriage. That incident taught me to learn as much as I can about each child.

STORY FROM A TEACHER

Ms. Kathey Ramos, 1st grade

At my school, the first contact we have with our students is when we look at the information card that the families fill out at registration. I go over those cards with a fine-tooth comb. I look for the child's name and nickname, the emergency numbers to see who their friends are, the siblings so I'll know how many are in the family, etc. I list everyone's birthday so I can see who is the youngest, oldest, etc. I check the birth order of the children as well. You'd be surprised how much I learn by studying those cards.

different addresses, you would know that there is the possibility that they are divorced or separated. By looking at the list of emergency contacts, you get an idea of the people whom this family trusts.

FINDING TIME EVERY DAY FOR EACH CHILD

Young children need time and attention from the adults who care for them. Finding time to interact with each child one-on-one is easier said than done. With so many children in a class, it is hard to find time when all the children are engaged in an activity so you can talk directly with just one child. Probably the easiest time to talk with just one child is during morning arrival time. Children's arrival times into the classroom tend to be staggered. Take advantage of this and use the first few minutes of the school day to talk to children individually. The chat may be little more than asking a child about his or her morning or the previous evening's events, but these brief individual conversations help establish a relationship between you and your students. These conversations also provide information about the child and his or her family that might be difficult to learn otherwise.

As the harried first days of school progress, it is easy to overlook some children, usually the quietest, most compliant children. The children who do not demand your

attention need your time and interest just as much as the children who always have a contribution to make to class discussions and ask lots of questions, or whose behavior demands your attention. Making systematic notes or keeping anecdotal records about each child is one way to address this issue.

After the first day of school is over, it is a good idea to sit down with your class roll and record three things that you know about each child. For this first time, it helps to focus on things you know about the child and/or family. If you cannot list three things, then focus on that child (or those children) during the next school day. On successive days, add to your list, changing the focus to academic achievements or behavior. Recording your observations of children in different settings—working in the classroom, eating in the cafeteria, playing at recess, etc.—helps create a broader picture of each child.

To help you get to know your students, consider varying the way you arrange the small groups in your classroom. At different times during the day, you may pair the quieter children with the more talkative ones, group the quiet children with other quiet children, or noisier ones with other talkative children. By observing children in these different situations, you soon learn which grouping works best for each child. But keep in mind that young children's needs change as they develop in academic areas as well as in social and emotional areas.

USING LANGUAGE TO MEET CHILDREN'S NEEDS

In early childhood classes, children have just as many social and emotional needs as they do academic ones. Early childhood educators recognize this fact and purposefully use language to calm upset children, reassure those filled with anxieties, and support the fearful ones. The reassurance that "I am here to help you. Together, we can find a way to help you feel better. Now let's think about this situation" is often all that a child needs.

Sometimes, using language to meet children's needs means helping them verbalize those needs. Family members who know children well can often respond to meet a child's needs even before that child has uttered a word. Parents are often attuned to their children and meet many needs as a matter of course. For example, a mother hears a sniffle and provides a tissue before the child's nose even begins to run. When these children come to school, they often do not know how to ask for the things they need. They may not even know what it is that they need. They just know something is wrong.

STORY FROM A TEACHER

Ms. Maria Cardona, kindergarten

For Susan, the beginning of school marked a difficult separation from her mother. During the first week, Susan cried every morning as her mother left, but as the week progressed she seemed to get more comfortable at school. Then came Thursday afternoon—Susan was tired and grouchy. As we walked back to the classroom from PE, all of a sudden she started sobbing. I went over to her, asking, "Susan, what's wrong?" "I'm only five. My mommy doesn't let me go to malls by myself," was her heartfelt response. I smiled at her and offered comfort. I had not thought of school from that point of view—she was feeling alone and scared, afraid of the school's space, which seemed as big as a shopping mall to her, and she didn't know how to ask for help with the problem.

By specifically teaching language that children need at school, you help children learn how to take care of their own needs. For example, when two children have a disagreement over an object, it would be easy to say, "James had this first. You are supposed to share, so he gets it while you play with this toy." But the learning for the children becomes more powerful when they are involved in finding a solution and implementing it. Sometimes the phrases children need to know are simple social courtesies, such as "please" or "thank you." They may need to know how to join a group or settle their differences. By teaching children these social phrases, you are giving them words to use to solve their own conflicts.

Positive TEACHER TALK

Sample Social Phrases to Help Children Deal With School Situations

★ "I don't like it when you _____. Will you please stop?"

★ "When you _____, I feel _____ (sad, mad, hurt, etc.). Will you please stop?"

★ "Excuse me, I was _____. Can you cooperate with me please?"

★ "You can use this after I finish. Thanks for waiting."

★ "I'll wait while you _____. Then I'll have a turn."

★ "Let's be lunchroom friends today and sit together."

★ "That game looks fun. Can I play?"

★ "I can _____. Would you like me to show you how to _____?"

★ "May I go to the restroom?"

Sometimes teachers use nonverbal communication with their children. A particular squinting of your eyebrows or look on your face can convey a thought more powerfully than words can. While every teacher needs to develop a "teacher look" that is similar to a "mom look" or a "dad look," it is also important to establish some other nonverbal signals as well. A clap-clap, clap-clap-clap can mean "line up" or "come here." Practice until you can do this loudly—a clap made with palms slightly cupped carries farther

than your voice can yell. Teach children what this signal means and what response is expected from them.

Children need opportunities to practice the response expected of them. Practice during the first few days of school before you actually use this signal. For example, before leaving the room for recess time, gather children in the group meeting area. Remind them that the clapping sound is the class's special signal to line up or that you may use it in an emergency. Lead children to practice "zooming their eyes" to you when you clap. Then role-play the situation by asking children to scatter themselves around the room, pretending to be playing at recess. Clap and motion for the children to line up. Most children readily follow this command when they are inside, but while they are outside engrossed in play, it may be a different story. Suggest to them that it is hard to listen for your clap when they are playing, and give some suggestions (check with friends in the class, glance at you while playing, etc.). Then tell children that you will "clap the signal" once during recess as a practice for lining up. After a short portion of the recess time has passed, clap the signal and motion for children to line up. Briefly describe the good things about their "lining-up behavior," then send them off to play again. If there are children who do not respond to a signal, speak to them individually. They may need extra reminders or consequences for not complying.

Guiding Children as They Make Activity Decisions

Learning to choose from among all the choices at school can be overwhelming for some children. Clearly explaining the choices and using carefully chosen language help them make these choices. We begin by offering children a limited number of activities. Then, as they are ready, we gradually increase the number of choices.

Most activity decisions are made at center time or other free-choice time. Early childhood teachers use a variety of management techniques to help organize children's choices. One way is to write each child's name on clothespins, list the choices (or available centers) on a chart, and then attach the clothespin beside the child's choice. Sometimes the number of children that may make that choice is indicated on the chart. Some teachers use dot stickers to indicate how many can participate or space the choices so there is just enough room for the correct number of clothespins to fit. Choices can also be managed with a grid that has children's names on one side and activity choices along the top. Children (or the teacher) follow the coordinates to fill in the square to indicate their choices.

At the very beginning of the school year, we offer children who have some difficulty making decisions only two choices—choice A or choice B—and we always tell them that whatever they choose, the other option is available on subsequent days. We might say, "Would you like to go to the science center or the explorations center today? Today you can pick one center, and tomorrow you can go to the same center or pick a different one."

Creating Opportunities for Children to Practice Respectful Language

Teachers need to create opportunities for children to practice the respectful language they are learning. The language of good manners—"please," "thank you," and "you're welcome"—is easily practiced during snack time. For example, as children are served their snack, they can reply, "Thank you." Or after finishing a snack, children can thank the person who provided the snack, saying, "Thank you. I enjoyed that snack today."

The give-and-take of respectful conversation can be practiced during any sort of work with a partner. Children can choose a partner, or you can assign pairs to read to each other, to play a math game, or to create a piece of artwork together. If you discuss some examples of respectful phrases that are appropriate for the upcoming activity, children are more likely to use respectful language. For example, if children are going to play a math game, you might suggest phrases such as these:

★ "Where would you like to sit to play our game?"

★ "I would like to sit by the door. Is that okay with you?"

★ "Let's decide together who is going to keep score."

★ "Please hand the dice to me."

★ "You went first last time. I think it is my turn to go first."

★ "It is okay; I do not mind."

Children who are taught specific phrases and given multiple opportunities to practice them are likely to incorporate them into their conversations. When children forget and use language that is disrespectful—and they will—reminders of previous conversations about respectful language are all most children need.

Teaching respectful language and providing children with opportunities to practice using it do not automatically eliminate all disrespectful language from the classroom. Changing habits is difficult, even for young children. When they are in the habit of speaking to their peers in a certain way, it is not easy to remember and use the respectful language they have been taught. This is a process that takes time, but it is well worth investing time in it early in the school year.

Cultivating Friendships Among Children

From the very first day of school, we work to cultivate friendships among children in the class. After all, this particular group of children is lumped together for an entire school year—friends or not. Things go much more smoothly when children view one another as friends. Some children naturally develop friendships with most of their classmates; however, many children need the teacher's help to understand what friendship is and how they should act toward friends.

As mentioned earlier, one way to foster this attitude among a group of children is to address the class in general as "friends." When you interrupt the class's work to give instructions or call for their attention, begin by saying, "Friends . . ." and then give the needed information. This sets the expectation that the children are friends and, thus, will act accordingly. The same is true for addressing children as "ladies and gentlemen," and so on.

Calling attention to an act of friendship you observe is another way to cultivate friendships and friendly behavior. When you observe a child sharing a pencil with another child, say, "Friends, I just saw the neatest thing. Calvin and Keanna are such friends! He had a pencil and shared it with Keanna. Isn't that a friendly thing to do?" By responding in this manner, you are labeling a particular behavior as the "behavior of friendship" and encouraging it. Many young children have never really considered what people do to show their friendship, so labeling these behaviors helps children begin to think about—and perform—acts of friendship.

Another way to establish friendships among children is to place them in small-group situations in which they can get to know one another. For example, if you organize your math manipulatives in small tubs, four or five children can easily gather on the floor to share the materials from one tub. One child can be responsible for getting needed materials and returning them to where they belong when the game is over.

Before children begin to work in small groups, you need to lead a class discussion about expected behaviors, and children should come to a consensus about what they think is acceptable behavior. After consensus has been reached (and these behaviors have been listed on chart paper for later reference), various children might role-play the expected behaviors while the others observe and comment on how well the actors demonstrated appropriate behaviors for small-group work.

A Classroom Conversation

A Second-Grade Conversation
About Working in Small Groups

Mrs. Ware: This afternoon we are going to work on our math a bit differently. You are going to do your math work with three other students. For the first three weeks of school, you have done your math work by yourself or with a partner. Today you are going to practice math skills by playing a game. I am sure you've worked in groups in kindergarten or first grade, but since we have not done that in second grade, I want us to make sure we understand what group work looks like in this class. So when I am walking around the room working with different groups, if I look across the room at your group, what will I see if your group is doing the right thing? Let's keep a list of the behaviors we agree on. I'll start by writing the title of this chart: "Appropriate Behavior for Math Games." Okay, who has an idea for what I should write first?

Justina: Being quiet.

Mrs. Ware: I think that is a good idea. May I write down "talk quietly"? That way, no one will disturb another group. So, I will watch for people talking quietly. What else?

Chen: Not fight.

Mrs. Ware: Now, fighting is definitely something I never want to see in this class. Sometimes you may have disagreements in your group and if that happens, you need to solve that disagreement with the conflict-resolution steps we use in this class. So, is it okay with you, Chen, if I write down "use conflict resolution if needed"? This is good. Talk quietly. Use conflict resolution if needed. What else?

Joe: Don't yell.

Mrs. Ware: Joe, I think that one is covered under Justina's suggestion. Can you yell if you are talking quietly?

Joe: No.

Mrs. Ware:	Okay, then, do you agree that we don't need another guideline that says "don't yell"?
Joe:	Yeah.
Mrs. Ware:	Okay, what else?

[No comments from students]

Mrs. Ware:	Let me think. Would it be a good idea to put this on our chart? Work only on the math game. Can you decide to work on something different during math time?
Children:	*[in chorus]* No!
Mrs. Ware:	Okay, then, shall I write "work only on the math game"?
Children:	*[in chorus]* Yes!
Mrs. Ware:	Do we need to list any other behaviors?
Children:	*[in chorus]* No!
Mrs. Ware:	Well, I am not sure. Let's try this today with only three behaviors *[pointing to chart tablet, reading aloud]* . . . "Appropriate Behavior for Math Games: Talk quietly. Use conflict resolution if needed. Work only on the math game." Those are the things I will be looking for today during math time. Now, let me explain how this game is played. . . .

STORY FROM A TEACHER

Ms. Nancy Lott, 2nd grade

When I would try to divide my class into small groups, it seemed like all the behavior problems ended up in the same group. I couldn't think of a fair way to make the groups without assigning permanent small groups, and I wanted them to be more flexible than that. So I started asking one person to get the needed material and wait in a certain area of the room. That person became the leader of the group. Our room has obvious areas for small-group work so the first group goes by the writing center, the second goes by the puppet theater, and so on. This leader holds up fingers to show the "number" of his group. Then, I touch the heads of the children to assign them to a group. That way, I can shuffle the groups a bit and children get into groups more quickly.

After children have worked in small groups for a time, introduce partner activities as well. This forces children to talk to each other and collaborate to play the game. Remark about specific friendly behaviors you observe. Suggest to children that they might continue this "friendship" after the partner activity is over. For example, "Roger, you and Becky worked so well together to play Double Compare, you may want to play together at recess today." Neither child may have thought of playing together later, but after you make the suggestion, they usually agree. If not, suggest that they might play together "on another day." The seeds of friendship are planted and will blossom at the right time.

Sometimes certain children share a strong interest in the same activity. Two boys may enjoy baseball while two girls share a love of soccer. Sharing this information with the two families may facilitate the children getting together outside of school. Many friendships between families have started when their children were in school.

STORY FROM A FAMILY

Our family has been best friends with another family from our school since the boys were in kindergarten. It all started when the teacher casually mentioned to me that Jimmy liked to shoot baskets at recess and Jamison did, too. After that, both of our families enrolled the boys in a YMCA basketball program. We began to go get ice cream after the games, and our friendship developed from there. I'm glad the teacher made that comment to us. Otherwise, we probably never would have known about the common interest between Jimmy and Jamison.

STORY FROM A TEACHER

Ms. Joy Box, 1st grade

At my school, children are not required to walk in a line when they are moving in the hall. We came to this decision as a faculty—after all, do adults ever walk in a line when they are moving in the hall? No, they learn to walk in small groups. In my class, we call this "walking with a friend." We practice the behavior and learn that you can walk close to another person, hold their hand, or simply walk in a group. Holding hands is really popular at first, but the novelty of that soon wears off. The children view this as a chance to be with someone they like instead of having to carefully control where they walk.

Teaching Collaboration With a Partner or in Small Groups

Much of the work our students do is with a partner or in small groups. While young children usually have played with one or more other children before coming to school, few of them have tried to work with peers to accomplish a specific goal or task. For partner work or small-group work to be successful, we need to teach appropriate behaviors and respectful language. As mentioned previously, we need to carefully explain what behaviors are expected for an upcoming learning experience and help children understand what to do when a conflict occurs.

Holding a class meeting to solve every conflict between children is not feasible. There is simply not enough time in the day. In fact, it is not desirable. We do not want to make solving problems the focus of every school day. So when two children or a small group of children are having problems getting along, we call a short meeting with just those children involved in the conflict.

At the beginning of the year, we are very directive in these meetings. We tell the children to look at each other, to talk to each other—not the teacher—and to respond to what the other person says. When any of the children involved is having trouble expressing him- or herself, we suggest language that he or she might use: "Are you angry or hurt? Then tell him, 'I am angry because you _____.' " Lots of times we repeat what one child has said: "Cassandra, Joley said that you hurt her feelings. Did you hear that? What do you want her to know about you hurting her feelings?" And we always conclude the meeting with an agreement: "It sounds like you guys are agreeing to _____. Cassandra, can you agree with this solution? Joley, can you agree with this solution? Okay, what is your plan now?"

Some problems are taken care of in one meeting. Once both parties understand what the other person was thinking, the whole issue is resolved. On the other hand, some problems recur, often involving the same two children. Some children need many discussions before they truly begin to see another person's point of view. It often takes many conversations before children begin to incorporate the language taught in conflict-resolution sessions into their independent interactions with someone they have a problem with.

STORY FROM A TEACHER

Ms. Katherine Sheffield, kindergarten

"Use your words." Many adults use this phrase with young children who show their anger or unwillingness to share through physical actions. This may be a good reminder phrase, but most of my students simply do not know what "use your words" means. When prompted to "use words," Jordan may yell, "IT'S MINE! I HAD IT FIRST!" In terms of creating a sense of community, yelling at someone is not any better than snatching the toy that is wanted. For quite a few weeks, I find I need to lead a conversation between the two children arguing over the toy. "Use your words" should be used only when children have been involved in lots of conversations about specific language the children are encouraged to use.

Resolving Conflicts With Pairs or Small Groups

★ "How did that make you feel?"

★ "Tell her exactly what she did that made you so _____ (angry, sad, etc.)."

★ "Did you hear what she said? Say what you heard her say."

★ "Do you understand what he meant? Tell me what he meant."

★ "Do you see the situation the same way he just explained?"

★ "Look at him when you are talking to him."

★ "Don't tell me. Tell him."

★ "Please use a normal voice."

★ "How does what he just said make you feel?"

★ "Did you mean to hurt him? Then tell him, 'I did not mean to hurt you.'"

★ "This sounds like a pretty serious problem. I wonder what you might do to solve this problem."

★ "Okay, together you came up with a number of possible solutions (list them). Which one do you think might be the best solution for the two of you?"

★ "What could you guys do differently next time so this problem doesn't happen again?"

Avoiding Common Teacher Talk Pitfalls

As mentioned in the first chapter, an important strategy for teaching children to use respectful language is the modeling that teachers do all day, every day. However, it is not easy to ensure that every utterance during the day is appropriate. Despite our best intentions, there are moments when we lapse back into language that was used with us when we were children. It is almost like replaying old tapes in our minds. Without really thinking about it, the language that we heard as elementary school children slips into our interactions with our own students. The only way to prevent this is to be consciously aware of the types of language that we want to use and the types of language that we do not want to use with children. The following sections are examples of the types of language we do *not* want to use with children.

CORRECTING ONE CHILD IN FRONT OF THE OTHERS

In social situations, it often seems one person stands out—usually with a negative connotation. In early childhood classrooms, the person who stands out is often the one who frequently misbehaves, makes bad choices, or generally calls attention to him- or herself. Calling attention to this child to correct his or her behavior generally exacerbates the situation.

One way of dealing with situations like this is to physically move closer to the child before talking to him or her. If you stand and walk calmly toward the child, bend over and whisper in her ear, she is less likely to continue to act out. After repeated redirection of a child, you may delay talking about the situation and simply indicate that the child should leave the group with a quiet, calm hand gesture toward the child's chair or another location in the room that is a bit more private. This gives the child a chance to calm down and reflect on the behavior.

Quietly removing a child from the situation until he or she calms down is one way to correct an individual child without the other children listening and watching. When the class's attention is focused on an activity, you can go to the misbehaving child and discuss the behavior.

Some teachers deal with individual children's misbehaviors with "behavior sheets." This simple grid (see page 60) has five sections, one for each day of the week. When a child continually misbehaves, you, the child, and the child's family may agree to use a behavior sheet. When the child repeats the misbehavior, calmly say, "Jamie, you are continuing to hit your friends. Our agreement is that you do not hit. Let's make a note on your behavior sheet." Then note the time of day along with a brief description of the behavior. At the end of the day, review the day's behaviors with the child and come up

Name _____

Week of _____

Monday	Tuesday	Wednesday	Thursday	Friday

with a general evaluation of the day. This general evaluation is often a happy face, straight face, or sad face. The child must have the sheet signed by a parent or guardian and then return it to school the next day. Using a behavior sheet focuses the child's attention on one behavior at a time and since young children often are not aware of their behaviors, brings each occurrence to the child's attention. This method is effective with some children but not with others. Unless this reinforcement appears to help a child use more appropriate behavior, it should not be used just to report inappropriate behaviors to parents.

USING GENERALIZATIONS

All too often, teachers find themselves making blanket statements to the entire class about the behavior of only a few children. Announcing, "You must stop talking in those loud voices. This class is out of control," is probably not true. While there are a few times when every child in the classroom is out of control or talking in a loud voice, usually making that kind of general statement is unfair to the minority of children who exhibit appropriate behavior. We need to stop and think about the implications of making such general statements. If a few children exhibit inappropriate behavior, then take the time to identify those children and speak only to them, not to the entire class.

HUMILIATING CHILDREN

When you have discussed a misbehavior with a child over and over, it is easy to become frustrated when the misbehavior continues. Some adults think that embarrassing a child or humiliating him or her causes the behavior to change. This is simply not true. Humiliating statements are not likely to be an effective method of getting children to behave more appropriately, and such statements can affect children for the rest of their lives.

It helps to avoid humiliating statements when you remember that one of your roles as a teacher is to help children learn more appropriate behaviors. Few adults use humiliation as a method to teach reading or math, so thinking of appropriate behavior as another subject to be taught can be a useful reminder.

Reminding Individual Students

We continually remind ourselves that we are working with young children. Just because we have discussed something in a class meeting or facilitated a conflict-resolution meeting with a small group of children does not mean that children automatically use those conversations to modify their language or their behavior. Some young children may not even remember those conversations from one day to the next.

Reminding children about respectful language and the conversations we had about different topics is part of the whole process of teaching respectful language. Depending on the child and the situation, sometimes we restate the agreement reached at the end

Reminding Children About Expectations

Repeating a Previous Agreement

"Cristianna, look at this chart. The title is 'Being a Good Listener.' Number one says, 'Look at the person who is talking.' Is that what you were doing in this morning's meeting when you were whispering to Breanna? What are you going to do in the next class meeting instead of whispering to friends?"

"You promised you would _____. But you broke your promise when you _____. What should happen now?"

Reminding Children of What They Said

"Jonathan, yesterday when you and Brian talked about playing soccer together, you agreed you would not push each other at all. Do you remember saying that? Okay, then I do not expect to see any pushing."

"Hmm, I remember two boys saying they could share these sand toys. Pulling on the sifter is not sharing. How can you change your behavior to show sharing?"

Asking Questions to Prompt Children's Memories

"Corey, do you remember what we agreed to do if we wanted to use the same math manipulatives that other people were using?"

"Look at our chart about behavior during silent reading time. See if you are doing happy-face or sad-face actions."

"Look in your journal to see what you wrote down about what to do when _____. Check your behavior."

of a class meeting or what was said at the end of a conflict-resolution meeting. Other times, we ask questions that prompt children to remember these words. For children who have continuing problems with a specific disruptive behavior, such as taking things from classmates, pushing peers out of the way, or yelling across the classroom, we often use the morning arrival time to remind that child about the behavior that is expected of him or her that day.

Summary

In setting the tone for the year, it is important to spend some time with each student every day and learn as much about each child as possible. The better you know your students, the more effective you are in teaching them. Early in the school year, help children learn to make decisions, use respectful language, develop friendships with classmates, and work with a partner and in small groups. Be careful about the language you use, always keeping in mind that your role is to help children learn more appropriate behavior.

CHAPTER
4

Helping Children Manage Their Behavior

A s discussed in previous chapters, the language teachers use helps set the tone for the year and establish a community of learners. That same language is also instrumental in helping children learn to manage their own behavior. Teachers use a variety of strategies to guide discussions about behavior and specifically teach problem-solving language. Children's books help children explore different topics related to how they interact with their peers. All this occurs in early childhood classrooms as teachers guide children to create criteria for classroom behavior, provide opportunities for children to practice appropriate behaviors, and teach children to assess their own behaviors.

Cooperatively Establishing Expectations for Behavior

All teachers agree that behavioral expectations must be established early in the year in any classroom (Denton & Kriete, 2000). Most early childhood educators define their role in helping children develop appropriate behaviors in terms of guidance rather than management or discipline. They view children's inappropriate actions as teaching opportunities rather than actions that require punishment. In child-centered classrooms, this approach offers necessary support for children as they develop self-control and removes the idea of "punishment" to atone for misbehavior.

STORY FROM A FAMILY

I'm a single mother with a first grader and a baby at home. I work long hours and when I get home, I am tired. When Olive's teachers contacted me about her bad behavior, I was not surprised. She had trouble in day care when she was little, and she always talks back to me when I try to tell her what to do.

But this teacher was different. She was telling me things that Olive did wrong, but she didn't want me to punish Olive for things she did at school. She wanted to talk with me about how Olive acted at home and to find out what was important to Olive. The teacher wasn't mad—she wanted to teach Olive other ways to act.

Mrs. Carlson suggested that at school she was going to talk to Olive about ways to cooperate with other children. She suggested that I use the same ideas to help her get along with her little brother. No one has ever talked to me about my problems with my kids before. I really appreciated that. And now Olive is doing better at school and at home.

Within a community of learners, we take the issue of guiding children's behaviors a step beyond child-centeredness. When expectations for behavior are established by children (with our guidance), these communities become child-directed, not just child-centered. That is, children are actively involved in making the decisions that shape the expected behaviors rather than just following "rules" presented by the teacher.

GUIDING BEHAVIOR DISCUSSIONS

In child-directed communities, our students develop and agree on guidelines that are reasonable and appropriate. We guide our students' discussions, but it is their voices that

are important. Of course, the paradox here is that behavioral expectations have to be established early in the school year, long before a group of children have learned to make decisions as a group. In fact, many young children have had no experience in classrooms where their opinions are solicited, much less valued. This process, the give-and-take of discussion and experimenting with possible solutions, is essential to learning how to get along in life. The teacher's leadership in these early class discussions about appropriate behavior is important (Perlmutter & Burrell, 2001).

A Classroom Conversation

A Kindergarten Class Meeting

Mr. Donald: I think we need to have a serious talk today about cleaning up at the end of the day. Some people are working very hard to put everything back where it belongs, but some people are not helping clean up at all. They just leave the center where they are working and start getting ready to go home. That is not fair. We all need to do our share of cleaning up. What do you guys think we should do about this problem?

Chelsea:	You could go around and tell people, "Clean up. Clean up."
Brock:	Or that could be a job for the job board.
Mr. Donald:	Those are two ideas for solving the problem, but let's think some more. Do you think that people in our class need someone telling them, "Clean up, clean up," every day?
Jonathon:	Yeah.
Demarrion:	Yeah, they do. If they aren't doing it, you got to tell 'em.
Mr. Donald:	Well, let's think about this. Instead of me walking around telling people what to do or making it one person's job to tell people what to do, how about all of us taking on the responsibility of reminding people. If any of us sees someone who is not cleaning up, we could say, "Remember, we all agreed to help clean up at the end of the day." What do you think about that?
Jonathon:	Yeah, that would work.
Julia:	We could do that.
Karen:	Yeah.
Mr. Donald:	Is this okay with everyone? Do you think you can remember to use the reminder words "Remember, we all agreed to help clean up at the end of the day" when you see someone not cleaning up? If you think this is a good idea and you think you can remember to do this, show me a thumbs-up. Great, I think we may have solved this problem. Let's meet again in a couple of days and see how this solution is working.

On the next page, you'll find some very direct statements for leading children into establishing rules. For example, you might ask, "How about this?" then state a rule in the format you think is best for the classroom. Or you might restate an overly long sentence more succinctly.

Discussing Appropriate Behavior in the First Few Class Meetings

★ "What behavior do we want to see?"

★ "Is that the way you want to be treated?"

★ "Should we check with some other classes to see what they do?"

★ "We have some serious work to do in this morning's meeting. We need to talk about how we want to be treated in this class."

★ "Sometimes people who want something from another person just yell, 'I want that. Give it to me.' How do you feel about all of us yelling at one another like that?"

★ "Juan, would you want Peter yelling at you if he wanted to _____? Brooke, how would you feel if Jennifer yelled that _____?"

★ "What words could we use to write that down?"

★ "One way to say it would be 'No _____ ,' but I'm wondering if there is a way to say what we should do instead of what we should *not* do."

★ "Can anyone think of something?"

★ "How about this—use a normal voice and say, 'Please may I _____?' or 'I want to _____, too. Can we do it together?'"

★ "How does that sound to you, Jorge? Cristianna? Brooke? Does everybody agree?"

★ "Okay, that's kind of a long sentence. What should I actually write down? Okay, watch my marker as I write, '_____.'"

At the beginning of the school year, we use these more directive statements, often along with the techniques of pondering and wondering aloud to guide class discussions (Diffily & Sassman, 2002). These two techniques allow you to help children when they are stuck due to their limited experience.

Pondering and wondering aloud are ways of guiding children's discussions without being overly directive with them. Pondering leads children into thinking more deeply about a topic, clarifying a point, or discussing nuances about a concept. Pondering statements include the following:

★ "I'm not sure. Who could we ask?"

★ "Hmm, really?"

★ "Now, that sounds interesting."

★ "Hmm, what do *you* think you could do?"

★ "I wonder where we could find that."

★ "What are our options?"

★ "How could we do that?"

★ "If that *is* happening, what could you do to make the situation better?"
(Diffily & Sassman, 2002)

The technique of wondering aloud can also be used to guide children's discussions. Here are some examples:

★ "Some people want to _____. Others want to _____. How can we decide what to do?"

★ "It seems to me that _____. Do you think we might _____?"

★ "I saw fifth graders who had a problem like this. They _____. Could we try that?"

★ "Doesn't your aunt know about _____? I wonder if she could help us."
(Diffily & Sassman, 2002)

To help reinforce the guidelines as the class agrees on them, create a wall display listing them (Denton & Kriete, 2000). Before children are accomplished writers, write the guideline on a sentence strip and ask children to draw pictures to illustrate what following that guideline would look like. As soon as children can express themselves in writing, they can take over that part as well.

STORY FROM A TEACHER

Ms. Jill Pham, kindergarten

From year to year, I always forget what it is like to have that first class meeting about how we are going to treat one another. The children's contributions to the discussion inevitably focus on what they should not do. Don't hit. Don't fight. Don't push. Don't call people names. I try to get them to focus on how they want to be treated. I try to change their words to be more positive. Instead of saying, "Don't hit," I suggest that maybe we write down, "Use words to get your way." They don't really understand at first. The children are bringing rules from their previous experiences to those first few discussions. It takes days, sometimes weeks, for the children to get the fact that appropriate class behavior is found in doing the right thing, instead of not breaking the rules.

USING CHILDREN'S LITERATURE

Children's books provide opportunities to introduce conversations about guidelines within a community (Sapon-Shevin, 1999). Some are funny, with the characters getting into unusual predicaments, while others are poignant, with touching moments when a friend or teacher makes a difference in a child's life. The books listed on pages 71–73 can be used to begin a class discussion, focus children's attention on a particular problem, or introduce possible solutions to a problem the class has been experiencing.

Children's literature is a nonthreatening way to introduce different types of respectful language (Dalton & Watson, 1997). We often use books to introduce ways to handle negative actions or language and help children learn to deal with rejection, name calling, or teasing.

Following the read aloud, we use a variety of language-arts strategies. We may challenge our students to describe how they would feel if they were the character in the story. We follow up by either listing ways the conflict was handled in the story or completing a whole-class activity related to the story. Whole-class activities we use at different times include guiding children to write letters (or composing a whole-class letter) to the character, congratulating him or her for the positive choices that he or she made. We may use Venn diagrams or two-column charts to compare and contrast the characters' actions in two similar books. To emphasize the sequence of a character's actions, children can construct murals of the story. Sometimes we divide the class into small groups, with each group illustrating an event in the story. Then we paste these illustrations onto a long piece of mural paper and add captions. Children also put themselves in the character's shoes, writing pieces like, "If I was Oliver Button, I would . . . ." Children can also dramatize the story, perhaps in a simple reader's theater or impromptu format. Many language-arts strategies are applicable here.

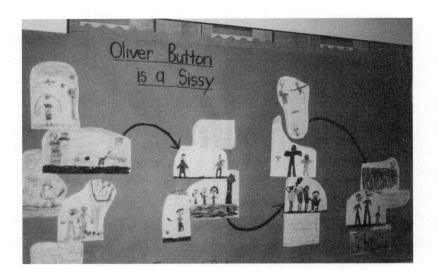

For Starting Conversations About Class Guidelines

Miss Nelson Is Missing by Harry Allard (Houghton Mifflin, 1984)
When the children in Room 207 become unmanageable, Miss Viola Swamp, the meanest, strictest substitute teacher in the world, takes over for Miss Nelson. The children soon realize the error of their ways and try to get Miss Nelson back.

. . . .

If You're Not Here, Please Raise Your Hand by Kalli Dakos (Aladdin, 1994)
This collection of poems offers a humorous glimpse into life in a school. Children will chuckle at the various predicaments that are presented.

. . . .

The Art Lesson by Tomie dePaola (G. P. Putnam's Sons, 1989)
Young Tommy's artistic talents are encouraged by his family, and he looks forward to attending school so he can have real art lessons. But the art lessons come with limitations—only one piece of paper, only "school crayons," and only copying. Tommy works out a compromise with his teachers and, in a surprise ending, shows that he is still drawing today.

. . . .

Next Year I'll Be Special by Patricia Reilly Giff (Bantam Doubleday Dell, 1980)
Marilyn clearly articulates all the changes she wants to see in her school career. She is looking forward to second grade next year. She just knows second grade will be better than her prior experiences. She predicts it will be a time when Miss Lark, the teacher, never yells but offers Marilyn her choice of classroom jobs, a time when Marilyn moves from the bottom reading group to being the best reader.

. . . .

Spot Goes to School by Eric Hill (Puffin, 1984)
Spot goes to his first day of school and enjoys a variety of activities. Eric Hill's clear illustrations and lift-the-flap style offer support for the simple text. The various activities of Spot's class can be a springboard for class discussion. For example, when children "start with a little song," Spot hides under the table because he can't sing. Children can discuss what Spot and the other children can do to make the

Continued next page

situation better. Or, use the page on which Spot and his friends play in the home center to develop guidelines for the class's center time.

. . . .

The Day the Teacher Went Bananas by James Howe (Dutton, 1984)
Even though he was a bit unconventional, the new teacher showed the children many things in just one day of school. At the end of the day, the principal solves the mix-up but the children find a way to stay close to their favorite teacher. Lillian Hoban's illustrations add to the charming text.

. . . .

Lunch Bunnies by Kathryn Lasky (Little, Brown, 1996)
Clyde is worried about his first lunch of first grade. His older brother Jefferson doesn't help any as he gives unsolicited advice on the consequences of spilling soup, describes mystery goosh, and warns about the behaviors of Gloria, old Mrs. Twig, and Francis, the lunch ladies. Clyde dreads meeting Gloria and is afraid he will spill his tray. In the end, Clyde helps a new friend with her spill and doesn't fear lunchtime anymore.

. . . .

Thank You, Mr. Falker by Patricia Polacco (Philomel, 1998)
In her autobiographical story, Patricia Polacco presents Trisha's difficulty with learning to read. Her difficulties are compounded by the teasing and taunting she endures in elementary school. A kind teacher, Mr. Falker, recognizes the problem and teaches her to overcome it. Children identify with Trisha's torment and feelings of inadequacy.

. . . .

Ruby the Copycat by Peggy Rathmann (Scholastic, 1991)
Ruby, the new girl, cautiously enters Miss Hart's class and takes a seat behind Angela. In an effort to fit in, Ruby goes to great lengths to copy everything that Angela does. Angela doesn't like it and writes Ruby a note to tell her. Ruby talks to Miss Hart and realizes that she has talents to share with the class that are uniquely her own.

Continued next page

Literature LINKS

Lunch Money and Other Poems About School by Carol Diggory Shields
(Puffin, 1994)
The poems in this book address aspects of school in a humorous way. Children
enjoy comparing their school's rules with the playground rules in "Recess Rules."

. . . .

Annabelle Swift, Kindergartner by Amy Schwartz (Orchard, 1988)
Lucy, Annabelle's big sister, teaches her all she needs to know about kindergarten.
But when Annabelle goes to kindergarten she finds out that Lucy's teachings were
not always correct. Everything works out in the end, when Annabelle is the only
kindergartner who can count the milk money.

. . . .

The Teacher From the Black Lagoon by Mike Thaler (Scholastic, 1989)
A boy's first-day-of-school worries about what his teacher will be like translate into
an amusing text. He thinks Mrs. Green is green and has a tail. Mrs. Green takes care
of any problems in the class by breathing fire on Freddy, unscrewing Eric's head,
and zapping Randy into a frog. This book sparks conversations about how children
want their teacher to act and how they should respond to her.

Creating Criteria Together

We do not expect young children to change immediately just because we hold a
class meeting about a particular inappropriate behavior. Even when children
come to an agreement on group expectations for behavior, we know they will not
suddenly begin acting in accordance with it. Young children need more than a one-time
discussion. They need someone to explain—several times—what each agreement
means. Even though children feel more ownership when they are involved in the
process, it still takes multiple conversations, demonstrations, and opportunities for
practice before most children learn to apply the norms most of the time.

When you help children develop criteria for certain behaviors, you really have to
question them fairly directly. During that first week of school, we focus on how to be a
good listener. That is hard for young children, since they are much more inclined to

want to talk than listen. Remembering that children don't see the components of a particular behavior until you help them, you know you need to ask lots of questions during those early class meetings. To get at the heart of establishing criteria for being a good listener, we lead directive discussions. An example is given below:

A Classroom Conversation

A First-Grade Class Meeting

Mrs. Woods: Let's all look at Cassie. She is being a good listener. Let's all look very closely to see what she is doing.

Jordan: Nothing.

Mrs. Woods: Look at her body. Is she facing me? I am talking and Cassie moved her whole body to face me. Can everyone do that? Okay, let's write down, "Move your body to face the person talking."

Mrs. Woods: Look at Cassie's eyes. What is she looking at?

David: Cassie is looking at you.

Mrs. Woods: Right. Should I write, "Look at the person who is talking"? Is that okay with you, Sheneka? How about you, James? Does "Look at the person who is talking" sound like something that should be part of the criteria for being a good listener? So, is this wording okay with everyone? *[Only after children indicate that they agree does the teacher write the phrase on the chart tablet.]*

Let's look at Cassie again. Cassie, we can't see what is going on in your brain. Can you tell us what you are thinking about while you are facing me and looking at me?

Cassie: My brain is thinking about what we are talking about.

Mrs. Woods: Okay, should we add "Think about what the person is saying" to our chart? Is this sentence okay with everyone? Let's read over the three criteria we listed for being a good listener. I'll read a sentence first, and then all of you echo read it. *[Reads all three statements.]*

I think you've made a good start here. We may want to look at this chart again in a few days to see if there are any other behaviors we should add to our list about being a good listener. For now, let's practice doing all three things that a good listener does. Move your body to face the person talking. I can see everyone facing me. Thank you. Now, look at the person who is talking. That would be me. Good, I can see all of your eyes looking at me. Now, think about what the person is saying. I am talking about being a good listener. Are you thinking about being a good listener? I can tell from the way you are practicing our criteria that you all are going to be very good listeners this year.

Discussions such as the one Mrs. Woods held continue throughout the year as new behaviors need to be discussed. Obviously, there are more of these discussions in the first few weeks of school, but there are times later in the school year when these discussions are appropriate. For example, if the class goes on a field trip to see a live performance, you need to lead a discussion about appropriate behavior for being a respectful audience; if the class takes on a service project, you need to lead a discussion about the appropriate way to interrupt an ongoing class.

Establish criteria for children's behavior, as a class and individually. This may seem overwhelming, but many of the criteria overlap. For example, the criteria for getting along in the room are the same as for getting along in the cafeteria. Hold class meetings to discuss any changes, adaptations, or new decisions that need to be made.

Providing Opportunities for Children to Practice Good Behaviors

After discussing behavioral expectations and writing down criteria that describe exactly what that behavior looks like, the class is ready for the next essential step in the process. Young children need multiple opportunities to practice a newly defined behavior. Practice reinforces the behavior and practicing it as a group reinforces children's commitment to one another. They help one another learn the agreed-upon guidelines and can remind one another in appropriate ways.

Some behaviors need to be practiced in a whole-class situation. For example, practicing transition times in the classroom and moving about the school building needs to be done as a whole group. In these situations, children learn to "do the right thing" as they repeat the task as described in their established guidelines and criteria. They also observe as other children practice the same task.

Katherine, beginning of 2nd grade

At my old school, we had rules like "no talking at lunch" and "keep hands, feet, and objects to yourself." They were kind of not good rules. I think we should be able to talk at lunch. At my new school, the teachers just say, "Act like you would in a restaurant." And at my new school, no one ever tells me to stop touching my friend. At my old school, it was always "keep hands, feet, and objects to yourself," "keep hands, feet, and objects to yourself," even if you weren't bothering your friend.

Begin practicing soon after the class has established the guidelines and criteria. If time permits, directly follow the decision-making time with practice time. If not, practice later in that same day. To begin practice time, we gather children in the meeting area and reread the criteria from the chart. Then we lead children in a discussion about "how the behavior looks." This might be a description of exactly how to push in chairs, get items from a locker, or line up at the door. We encourage children to explain in detail every aspect of the behavior and point out how each child is responsible for his or her own behavior.

After we have discussed the details, children practice the behavior, demonstrating the right way to accomplish the task. Since the whole class participates together in this exercise, children feel a sense of responsibility to help one another remember the criteria. Afterward, we gather back in the group area to critique the practice. This process may seem time-consuming. Initially, it does take some time, but making sure that everyone in the class understands the guidelines and criteria saves lots of reminder discussions through the rest of the year. Think of the time spent as an investment.

Make sure all children understand the rules and/or guidelines in the same way. For example, to the adult mind, "line up for lunch" is a very straightforward request, but that statement could mean different things to different

1. Get your lunck box
2. Get in lin
3. walk slow
4 ceep your hads to your self
5. walkin the cafrtered
6. walk to your tabal

children. Teachers expect children to stop talking, get up from their tables, push in their chairs, walk quietly toward the door, get what is needed for lunch, stand behind the last child in line, and wait quietly for the next direction. Young children may see no need to stop talking, to walk—much less walk directly toward the door—or to wait quietly. The child who forgets to push in his chair, wanders by the science area to check out the guinea pig, remembers that he forgot his lunch money, swings by his locker to get it, realizes that he wants to be in the front of the line, runs through a group of other children, and pushes to get to the front may honestly believe that he is "lining up for lunch."

Other times that may call for whole-group practice include common group activities such as playing on the playground. We gather for a class meeting on the playground and then "go play" to try out the behaviors of teacher and children. The attitude of "is this working?" continues during this time and the practice session is evaluated at the end of the play period. During the practice time, we monitor children's behaviors, walking around and asking them, "How are you doing? Is it fun to play without hitting? Can you think of something that would make our recess time better for everyone?"

So that everyone in the community—the teacher and all of the children— understands exactly what their agreed-upon expectations mean, we go through the same process for every guideline. We agree on a guideline, discuss and record criteria that describe the behavior in detail, role-play what that behavior looks like, and practice that behavior, following the established criteria.

Another way to practice a new behavior or routine is to ask a group of three or four children to demonstrate it for the class. After this small group role-plays the situation, the rest of the class discusses what the children did correctly and how they would improve or change their behavior. At this point, the other children may practice the behavior in this new manner.

These small-group demonstrations can be spontaneous, such as, "I just noticed how this table of children cleaned up their pencils, markers, and paper. Could you do that again while the rest of the class watches?" Or it can be practiced, such as, "Carley and Ramon, when we have our group meeting today could you show everyone how to share a book for partner reading? Go back by the puppet theater and practice. I'll check with you before we have the group meeting to see if you need any help."

Sometimes the process can be even more directive as you suggest to children exactly what to say and do, such as, "We've been having a few problems coming to our meeting area and getting settled. Josh, Jordan, and Breanna, please go stand by the science center. When I give the come-to-a-meeting signal, would you walk slowly to the meeting area, and Josh, would you pretend you cannot find a place to sit? Would you say, 'Breanna, please make a place for me'? Then the whole class can see what to do."

Conversely, a small group of children can demonstrate inappropriate behavior. Then the discussion centers on ways to improve the situation. Sometimes observing inappropriate behavior is the most effective strategy. Young children can often spot the "bad" behavior—and think of ways to change it—quicker than they can spot good behavior, not to mention the fact that young children love the humor associated with demonstrating inappropriate behavior.

A Classroom Conversation

Mrs. Gillmer's Kindergarten Class Meeting
About Practicing a New Routine

Today we are going to change the way we do our writing time. Instead of a student handing out paper to each person and table leaders handing out writing folders, each person will be responsible for getting his or her own. So, I need everyone to listen and watch me go through the new routine for writing workshop. Are you ready? When I see everyone's eyes on me, I'll know you are ready.

Okay, when I look into your eyes and nod at you, you will know that it is your turn to stand up and walk over here *[walks to drop file container]* and get your writing folder. You need to think about what color your folder is and whether your name is written on the middle tab or one of the end tabs. That helps you find your folder quickly. Next, you walk to the writing center *[walks to writing center]* and get a piece of paper. Then, you walk to this bookshelf *[walks to bookshelf]* and date stamp your paper. Finally, you choose where you want to write that day. If you want to sit at a table, that is still fine. You can get a pencil from the basket on that table. If you want to sit on the floor, you need to stop by a table *[continues to model]* and get a pencil, then walk to the clipboard basket and get a clipboard. Now, you have what you need to start writing.

Please remember, when you are choosing a place to write, you need to think about where you can be the most serious writer that day. If that place is the floor, that is good. If that place is a table, that is good. So as soon as you have your writing folder, a date-stamped paper, a pencil, and possibly a clipboard, you need to start writing. And that is our new routine for writing workshop. Those are a lot of things to remember, so we need two volunteers to demonstrate the routine as I talk it through one more time. Who volunteers? *[Selects two children.]*

Okay, watch for me to look at you and nod. I'll give you word clues and you go through the routine. Okay *[nods at first child, then second child]*. Writing folder . . . *[pauses between each step]* . . . paper . . . date stamp . . . pencil . . . clipboard . . . place in the room to be a serious writer.

Thanks! I think that was pretty good. What do you guys think? *[Allows two or three children to comment on how the volunteers did.]*

Okay, who is ready to role-play this routine one last time before we all try it? *[Chooses four or five volunteers.]* This time we will all help them with the five steps by saying each step. Remember *[holds up fingers for the steps, one through five]* . . . paper . . . date stamp . . . pencil . . . clipboard . . . choose a place. Volunteers, are you ready? Class, are you ready to help them by calling out the steps? Let's go *[nods at the volunteers one at a time]* . . . paper . . . date stamp . . . pencil . . . clipboard . . . choose a place *[holds up fingers for the steps, one through five]*.

How did they do? *[Allows two or three children to comment on how the volunteers did.]* I agree. They did very well. They remembered what each step looked like. Maybe if one of them forgot a step, he or she could look at the person ahead for a clue on what to do next. That might be a good idea for you to think about.

I think we are ready to try out our new writing-workshop routine. Remember, one, two, three, four, five . . . paper . . . date stamp . . . pencil . . . clipboard . . . choose a place. Now, watch me and when I nod at you, it will be your turn.

Ms. Kelly Mercer, 2nd grade

Some of my colleagues make fun of me during the first couple of weeks of school, in the hall, in the library, in the cafeteria. Wherever they see me, I'm leading my students through some kind of practice. I truly believe that if you teach your students the routines during the first month of the school year, then you spend a lot less time during the other eight months dealing with behavior issues. I talk to children about each routine and take the time to write each step of the routine on chart paper or in our class book. Too often, teachers think their students understand what they mean when they announce, "I expect appropriate lunch behavior." When you stop and think about it, we expect a lot from children while they eat their lunches. So after we've talked about our lunch routine, we take our list of expected behaviors and go to the cafeteria to practice:

★ walking down the hall without disturbing other classes,

★ waiting quietly in line,

★ making decisions about food choices before reaching the food,

★ pulling a poem out of a pocket to read if you get bored,

★ walking through the lunch line,

★ asking for lunch items loudly enough to be heard,

★ saying thank you to the people serving lunch,

★ having the lunch card readily available when you get to the cashier,

★ choosing where to sit,

★ using polite language to ask if a certain place is free,

★ talking in quiet voices,

★ using good table manners,

★ gathering trash after eating,

★ walking around the other classes to get to the trash cans,

Continued next page

★ depositing the trash properly (recycling the plastic and cans), and

★ joining the class at the line-up area.

Even after all this discussion and practice, "using good table manners" usually develops into its own list of desired behaviors. Since our guidelines are written down, we can go back and review them as needed. I try to watch for breakdowns in the behaviors and review our lists before things get out of hand. Children are children and need reminders about what is appropriate. So we just practice again.

STORY FROM A CHILD

Marques, beginning of 1st grade

My favorite part of group meetings is when I get to act bad. Everybody looks at me and says what I should do instead of being bad. Then I do the good things they say. It is fun.

Teaching Children to Self-Assess Behaviors

When a problem arises, we first review the established criteria with the whole class. This means simply rereading the list of behaviors and explaining again what is expected. This occurs often at the beginning of the year. Sometimes criteria need a bit of tweaking to make them fit a new situation, or something may need to be added.

If a problem continues, we ask children to role-play the situation—dramatizing the inappropriate behavior as well as the appropriate way to follow criteria. As a group, children offer suggestions about why a behavior is inappropriate for the classroom. Children often remind one another why a particular guideline was established. The process of critiquing behavior reminds children about previous conversations. Usually, this translates into more children following the guidelines.

Leading children into making these class guidelines seems difficult at the time. However, it often turns out to be the easy part of developing a child-directed community. Helping children apply the criteria to their daily routine is the hard part. We remind children of the criteria and note when they are "doing the right thing." Recognizing children who follow the established guidelines reminds the rest of the class about what they decided (Kriete, 1999). We need to be careful that the language we use recognizes children's specific acts, rather than dispensing general praise (Kohn, 1996). Phrases such as "I really like that," "Good job," or "I'm so proud," quickly lose any meaning. True recognition is:

★ **authentic:** based on genuine accomplishments that occur every day;

★ **personal:** based on participation and choices of students;

★ **inclusive:** available to all students without condition;

★ **varied:** provides infinite opportunities for recognizing students' successes" (Cameron et al., 1997, p. 8)

STORY FROM A TEACHER

Ms. Krystal Jackson, 1st grade

I overheard Emily and Shawne as they worked in the painting center. Emily, the conscientious rule follower, said, "Shawne, I remember when you used to spatter paint all over the floor. You're not doing that today." "Yeah," he grudgingly replied. "When we talked about it, I figured I'd just have to clean it up so I'm real careful now." Little snippets like this remind me that the time I spend working with children to get them to come up with guidelines for our class's operation is all worth it. Shawne changed his behavior because he decided to—not because I made him do it. That's a big step.

Positive

TEACHER TALK

Giving Recognition to Children Following Guidelines

Give specific feedback instead of general praise. Comment on specific behavior:

★ "I noticed how quickly and quietly you came to the meeting area this morning."

★ "I saw many people remembering to smile at one another when you came into class this morning."

★ "Thank you for being a good listener. It makes other people feel good when you listen carefully to what they are sharing."

★ "John Robert, you handed that book to Richard just like we practiced."

★ "Wow! I am seeing children who remember how to get their snack from the snack table in a polite way."

★ "I appreciate how you remembered to ask your friends for something you want and use the word 'please.' When I hear you say, 'May I please borrow your glue?' that makes me so proud of you."

Summary

Teacher language is just as important a part of helping children learn appropriate behaviors for school as any other. Children are more likely to use appropriate school behavior when they have a part in developing those expectations. This can be done through class discussions about behavior, direct teaching, and the use of children's literature as a springboard for such discussions. Criteria need to be created for each behavior. Also, children need opportunities to practice good behaviors and they need to learn to self-assess their own behavior.

Teaching Language for Specific Situations

Some situations are common among all early childhood classrooms—asking an adult for help, cooperating with peers, joining a group, and resolving conflicts. To varying degrees, these same situations are encountered all throughout school—and throughout adult life as well. For children to learn how to handle these situations, we teach them specific language to use. An additional benefit is that a sense of community develops when everyone understands and uses the same phrases.

At some point, every child in the class vies for the teacher's attention. Several phrases are appropriate in this situation, in part depending on your preference and in part on the school's expectations. By sharing these preferences with children, you give them a chance to learn how to respond in an appropriate manner. Another situation occurs when a child wants something from a classmate. Such incidents happen every day, sometimes several times a day. They can be simple or complex, ranging from a minor tussle over a toy to a full-scale confrontation that demands a modification of behavior patterns. Many children have learned inappropriate ways to get what they want from another child, so appropriate ways to address peers becomes a topic for discussion. Yet another situation occurs when one child wants to join a group of children who are already engaged in something. Young children need support in learning how to join in an activity in progress. More generally, children need to learn specific language to resolve conflict whenever it arises. This skill will benefit them throughout their lives.

Discussing each of these situations while suggesting and practicing specific language empowers children. They learn how to respond appropriately when you take the time to teach appropriate language and provide multiple opportunities to practice it. And the day goes more smoothly when common language is understood, expected, and used.

Helping Children Get What They Want From the Teacher

You know the situation—a child comes up to you, repeatedly tapping on your arm to get your attention or a child yells across the room, "Teacher, teacher!" This tapping-on-the-arm or tugging-on-clothes behavior can be annoying, and several voices raised together calling out, "Teacher, teacher" disturb the entire class. You are exhausted—pulled in a hundred different directions—and still children vie for your attention. Young children, especially those who have not been in large-group situations before, need to be taught specific behaviors to use to get your attention.

To prevent these annoying behaviors, begin by having honest conversations with the class, explaining that you wish you had time to listen to every single thing they want to tell you, but that you just cannot, that there are too many of them for you to always listen to what they want to tell you. You can suggest alternative ways of sharing stories with you—they could write a letter (or draw a picture), wait until an appropriate time, or relate their story to a friend.

Young children do not always want (or need) to share a specific "story," they just want to know that you have noticed them. So, in addition to making time for each child during morning arrival time, create opportunities for children to get individual attention. Individual writing (or reading, math, etc.) conferences offer children a regular, scheduled opportunity to have your undivided attention. Some teachers eat lunch with rotating groups of children, giving each child a scheduled time that is open for personal conversation. Other teachers use recess as a time for children to share stories with them or visit with children as they walk down the hall, wait in the restroom line, etc. Of course, these behaviors are specifically described and practiced, but by effectively using these snippets of the day, you are modeling ways to carry on a conversation and reinforcing the importance of each child.

Even after holding class discussions with children about your expectations for getting your attention, you still need to give reminders. Handle repeated, annoying attention-getting behaviors in a straightforward manner, directly describing the annoying behavior to the child. For example, if you do not want to be tapped on the arm, look directly at the child and say, "I do not like it when you tap me on the arm. Will you please stop?" Wait for a response from the child and say, "Thank you. I will listen to you when Charles finishes." This conversation models the behavior you want children to use with one another, reminds them to stop tapping you on the arm, and reassures them that they also get some time from you.

Conduct frank conversations with children about how you plan to offer attention to the class. You might say, "I know that sometimes you feel like you have to say something a lot of times before your mom or dad hears you. But I am your teacher and I am going to try really hard to listen so you have to say something only once. If you make sure that I am listening before you talk and watch for my response (a smile, a nod, a reply, etc.), then I will know what you said. Can we practice that now?" Sometimes children are accustomed to a verbal response and think that an adult has not heard them unless an oral reply is given. Children may not look directly at the person whose attention they are trying to get. It may be necessary to teach them to recognize a nod, a smile, or a raised eyebrow as an appropriate response.

Children who "need help" offer a different challenge. While you may reassure children that you will always help them when they need it, young children do not have the same sense of priority as adults. To a young child, "needing" a blue crayon and needing help to stop a bloody nose may have the same degree of importance. You may also want to explain that it may not always be possible for you to help children at the exact time that they decide they need help.

You also need to explain very carefully that the teacher is not the only person in a classroom who can answer questions—their peers or resources within the classroom can also help. Show children ways to help one another. For example, while you hold a conference with one child about his writing, another child may feel "stuck" until she can ask you for the /s/ sound. So she sits, off task until she can ask you about the sound. In this case, a more-proficient child could help her.

We work to establish interdependence among our students. This can be as simple as saying, "Jordan knows how to tie shoes. Ask him for help," or as complex as, "I'm not sure. Would Josh know how to look that up in the dictionary?" After this idea of "asking a friend for help" becomes established, a child can be named the "class expert" in an area in which he or she has particular skills. Other children know, without the teacher's intervention, to ask that child for help first. Some teachers list these experts on a chart tablet that includes every member of the class. The "expert" skills do not have to be academic; experts are also needed to remove a jam from the stapler, stack the wooden blocks in the right places, open the glue bottle, and so on.

Resources within the classroom can also offer children help. Young children do not notice charts or other things posted in the classroom unless you specifically call their attention to it. One way to approach this is to wait to post the chart until children need that skill. Then, introduce the skill with that chart and tell children to "check the chart when they forget." For example, when introducing letters of the alphabet, you might ask, "Would it be helpful if we had these letters somewhere in the room so you could

look at them when you forget if a *b* goes to the right or left? I have this ABC chart that we could put above the chalkboard if you think that would help." Then, in another lesson, you might say, "I found these cool ABC strips that are on sticky tape. They are small enough that I could put them on your tables and then you could look there for help or above the chalkboard. Is that a good idea?" If you prefer to have the charts posted before school starts, simply call attention to them when needed.

Directing children to go to other children for help or referring them to other easily available resources in the classroom fosters independence. Young children feel a sense of satisfaction when they solve a problem on their own, leading to a more positive outlook as well as proficient learning.

In a class meeting, we bring up the topic of what to do when you need help. We lead the discussion to form guidelines, creating a chart of appropriate behaviors. The chart in the photograph above shows guidelines developed by the kindergarten children in Charlotte's class.

While these kindergarten children thought of five things to do, other teachers use the "Rule of Twos." This means that a child has to try two ways to get help before asking the teacher. This could be asking two friends for help or referring to one of the class's references and asking one friend.

Ms. Kelly Mercer, 2nd grade

Charles always asked me the silliest questions. He'd ask, "Where's the paper?" just after I explained where the paper was located or "Can I use a marker?" just after I explained that only crayons would work for this particular task. It was annoying, to say the least. But then I looked a little further at his behavior and needs. I realized that he was looking for attention from me and the only way he knew how to get it was to ask a question. So he was asking every question that came to his mind! I started checking with him as I finished giving directions, saying, "Charles, do you understand what to do?" or "Charles, ready to work?" Just a little bit of special attention toward him changed his behavior. He was getting my attention in a constructive way now.

Helping Children Get What They Want From Peers

Typically, young children also need help learning how to ask for what they want from their peers. Grabbing the scissors out of another child's hand is one way to get the desired object. However, the child doing the grabbing doesn't get to keep the scissors long because the other child just grabs them back. And then, grabbing and arguing become the way to act.

Rather than waste time stopping the "grabbing and arguing," present language for children to use when they want something from another child. Children learn to ask in a respectful way, assuring that the object will be treated with respect and returned.

A group of second-grade children brainstormed this list of ways to get what you want from other people:

1. Ask in a polite voice, "May I use your pencil, please? I'll give it back."

2. Explain why you need the object: "My marker is dried up. May I use yours?"

3. Treat everything with respect so people will believe you.

4. Tell the person when you return the object, "Here is your marker."

5. Say thank you: "Here is your book. Thank you for letting me read it."

6. Offer a suggestion if you have to say no to someone: "Sorry, we are using that paper, but there is some more on the shelf that you could use."

Ms. Kathey Ramos, 1st grade

Why is it that the two children who can't get along together invariably seek each other's friendship? Aaron and Andy were such two boys. They wanted to be best friends but always ended up hitting, fighting, or calling each other names. When we had our class meeting about using I-statements, I thought that technique might help them. So I was disappointed when I saw them arguing over a car in the block center. After I asked what the problem was, I realized that they still just wanted to play together but didn't know how to share the toys. I suggested that they both say what they wanted, using the I-statement format. With a little prodding from me, they agreed to try saying, "I want the _____, please" or "May I use the _____?" before grabbing. I checked back with them frequently and stopped by for some closure at the end of center time. They were using the I-statements and, later in the year, learned to use them on their own.

Teaching such language reduces bickering among children, and the shared language instills a feeling of community among children. They begin to feel like their class is a special group of people. However, children do not automatically begin using this language simply because you introduce these phrases in one class meeting. First, share the phrases with children and then explain why they are to be used in this class. After that, structure opportunities for children to practice using the established phrases. During the meeting, you could suggest that children turn to a classmate and practice asking for something so that they get immediate practice with one of the phrases. At another class meeting, you might ask a few children to role-play appropriate ways to ask a friend for something. On another day, you could simply remind children to use one of the phrases when they wanted something from someone else. Over time, with reminders and opportunities to practice, children incorporate these respectful phrases into their everyday conversations.

Joining a Group

Often, young children who want to join a group of children already engaged in an activity do not know what to say or do. Some children are accustomed to their parents or teachers always telling them what to do. Others have never been in classrooms where group work was the norm. Some children have experienced rejection in past group experiences and assume it will be the same way in this class. Whatever the reason, many children simply do not know what to do when they want to join an ongoing activity. Often these children watch from a distance, hoping someone will notice them and extend an invitation. Others simply bluster their way into a group and try to take over. None of these strategies is particularly effective.

Group discussions and role-play are especially important in helping children learn the language of joining a group (Bickart et al., 1999). Different children in the class are learning different roles in these situations. Not only are the shy or inexperienced children learning the words to persuade other children to let them into their play, but the other children in the class are learning that when they hear certain phrases they need to make places for those children—or explain why it is not possible for one more person to join the group.

Teaching Children What to Say When They Want to Join a Group

★ "Introduce yourself to the group. Say, 'Hi! Can I play?' "

★ "Does it look like more children could be in that game (activity, table, etc.)? Ask, 'Is there room for one more?' "

★ "Make a suggestion to the people in the group. Say, 'Have you thought of _____?' "

★ "Ask about the rules before you play. Say, 'Who's it? I'll chase him too.' "

★ "Tell the person what you want. Say, 'I saw you playing in the sandbox. I like to do that, too.' "

★ "Let them know about your skills and strengths. Think to yourself, *How will those children know that I am an expert about* _____? They probably need your help. Could you offer your ideas without being bossy to them? Practice what you will say to them with me."

★ "If they say no, ask if you can participate on another day. Say, 'Okay, if you have enough people today, can I play tomorrow?' "

When helping children learn what to do to join a group, it is beneficial to enlist the aid of other children. For example, when you notice a particular child who appears reluctant to join a group or wanders alone on the playground, you might appeal to another child for help. For example, you might say, "Joey, it looks like Shannon needs a friend. She is not playing with anyone. Could you see if she wants to play with you in the sandbox?" or "Jimmy, Sean knows a lot about dinosaurs and he's not working with any group right now. Could you ask him if he wants to work with your group?"

Sometimes just easing the transition is all that is necessary for a child to successfully join a group. Most children are willing to allow other children into their activity. The next time this situation arises, the child may remember the words you used and mimic them, or he may remember the role-playing from a class meeting and use that language.

Resolving Conflicts

Class meetings are a good place to talk about the kind of language that supports a sense of community (Diffily & Sassman, 2002). Several different topics can be discussed under the umbrella of "ways we want our class to be." We find that many of the class meetings during that first month of school focus on resolving conflicts.

STORY FROM A TEACHER

Ms. Amanda Dunlap, 1st grade

I was used to solving every conflict for the children in my class. I told them where to sit, how to put their supplies away—really, I told them everything. Then I moved to a new school where the staff decided that recognizing children's voices in decision making was an important part of their learning. It was so, so hard for me—not for the children—but for me. I realized I'm kind of a bossy person and that I was just bossing the children around—and they weren't learning from the bossing. That staff was exactly right—the children learned so much more when I took the time to involve the children in making decisions, but it was so hard for me to bite my tongue and wait for the children to come up with a solution. Now, that comes second nature to me. I'm glad I changed—I know it is better for the children. And, hey, I'm working on not being so bossy with my husband and my own children as well.

Conflicts arise in all sorts of situations. Wherever there are people, there is inevitably conflict. This is certainly true in early childhood classrooms. Many of us are not comfortable with conflict and want to get it settled as soon as possible. Children's conflicts in the classroom often stir up other problems, so we want them solved quickly. Usually, the fastest way to end a conflict between children is to simply tell them what is best. However, when we solve the problem, we are not teaching children how to resolve conflicts (DeVries & Zan, 1994).

We do not try to avoid conflict or to end it with our own pronouncements. Conflict occurs within any group of people. Teachers of young children need to recognize this fact and help them learn what to do when a conflict arises. Children benefit the most when we help them understand conflict and what to do when it occurs. Perhaps the most difficult language to teach young children is the language of conflict resolution.

We use class meetings to teach the language of conflict resolution. At the beginning of the year in these conversations, we do not mention the names of children involved in conflicts or even refer to a specific conflict we observed. We use the time in class meetings to bring up conflicts in a more generic way, like "Do you know what happened in my class last year? There were two children who didn't know how to handle being angry. When they would get mad, they would call each other rude names. Can you believe that?" Inevitably children want to know what the "rude names" were. They respond with "oohs" and "aahs" when we whisper the word "stupid." That is generally enough to launch a conversation about how we feel when people call us names and what we can do when that happens. If there is sufficient time, we ask a few children to role-play some of the solutions the class developed. If time is short, we definitely return to this topic in another meeting.

On subsequent days, using another story, we bring up different conflicts. We teach children that resolving conflicts typically uses four separate stages:

1. Identifying the problem

2. Discussing how we would feel if we were involved in that situation

3. Brainstorming possible solutions

4. Role-playing one or more of the solutions

As the year progresses our discussion moves from generic problems and begins to address conflicts that are actually occurring among children in the class. We do not allow these meetings to embarrass any child. A conflict comes before the whole class only when both (or all) children involved in the conflict agree to present their

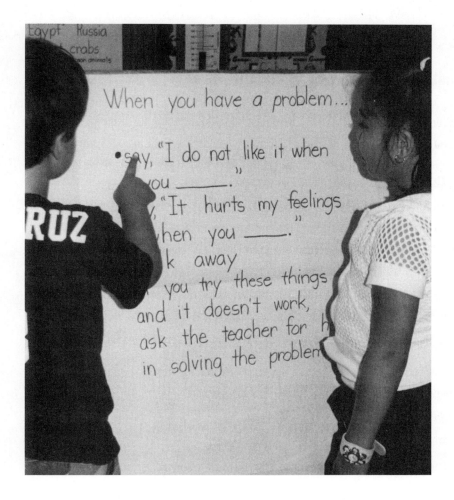

problem in a class meeting. Depending on the problem, these meetings can be handled in different ways.

The organization of a class meeting changes slightly when a conflict between two children is discussed. In these meetings:

★ the teacher summarizes the problem;

★ both children take a turn explaining their side;

★ children in the group have an opportunity to make suggestions about ways the children could solve the problem;

★ the two children involved leave the group, find a private place in the room, decide how they are going to handle their problem, and then report back to the whole group.

Mr. Jonathan Lintz, kindergarten

My kindergarten class and "the most beautiful rock in the world" helped with my understanding of conflict resolution. On our spring field trip to a farm, Jacob found a piece of white quartz and asked the landowner if he could have it. The farmer agreed and Jacob carried his rock with him for the rest of the day. Unbeknownst to anyone else in the class, Jacob's mother made him leave the rock on the playground when she picked him up that afternoon. The next day at recess, Clarissa found the rock and claimed it for her own. Both children truly believed they owned the rock. They asked to discuss their problem in the next class meeting.

Both children explained why that rock was theirs, and children in the class offered their evaluation of the situation and their advice. Among the comments were:

★ "The rock belongs to Jacob. He found it first."

★ "The rock belongs to Clarissa because Jacob's mom made him leave it here, and Clarissa found it first today."

★ "If they are going to argue about it, Jacob and Clarissa should not get to keep it."

★ "They could share the rock and take it home every other night."

★ "They could leave the rock in the science center."

Jacob and Clarissa went to the corner of the room for a moment. They returned to the group and announced their decision: They wanted me to cut the rock in half. While I knew this would not work, the children watched as I sawed a knife back and forth with absolutely no effect on the rock. After a full three minutes, Jacob said, "Well, this isn't working. Come on, Clarissa."

The two children went back to their corner, spoke for less than a minute, and returned asking me to hit the rock in half with a hammer. After I found a hammer in the custodian's closet, we all went outside. I covered the rock with a towel (so if it shattered when hit, the pieces would not hit anyone), and hit the rock as hard as I could. It broke into three pieces of quartz; one large piece and two small pieces.

Jacob announced, "Come on, Clarissa." They walked away from the group, exchanged a few comments, and then returned to the group. As serious as any child can be, Jacob declared he and Clarissa wanted me to keep hitting the rock until they had enough pieces of "the most beautiful rock in the world" so that everyone in the class could have their very own piece.

Solving the conflict over who owned the rock took longer than most problems. However, this story illustrates the importance of children feeling ownership of their own problems and the teacher taking the children's solutions seriously (even when he thinks the solution will not work).

"Tattling" can consume much of the learning time in early childhood classrooms. We want children to be responsible for their own actions—not to report misbehaviors of other children. We deal with this in a very straightforward manner, asking the child who has come to us to report a misbehavior, "How are you involved in that situation?" We continue to question the child until she understands that if she is not involved, then she should not be reporting it. These conversations usually go like the one below:

A Classroom Conversation

**A First-Grade Teacher–Student
Interaction on the Playground**

Jordan:	Ashleigh wants me to tell you that Jared hit her hand with a rock.
Mrs. Ware:	Jordan, how are you involved in this situation?
Jordan:	She wants me to tell you.
Mrs. Ware:	I appreciate that you are trying to help a friend, but how are you involved in this situation? Were you a part of the rock throwing?
Jordan:	No, I wasn't throwing rocks.
Mrs. Ware:	Hmm, were you hit by a rock that someone else threw?
Jordan:	No.
Mrs. Ware:	Okay, since this seems to be Ashleigh's problem, she can come and tell me that she needs help solving a problem. This is Ashleigh's responsibility, not yours. Do you understand?
Jordan:	Yeah.

The broken-record technique, repeating the same phrase, is quite effective here. It focuses the child's attention on the question at hand: "How are you involved?" Often the child who is involved watches to see how this interaction goes, and when the tattling child returns to report on "what the teacher said," she either comes to report the incident or lets it drop.

When several ways to solve conflicts have been introduced, we hold a class meeting to summarize the different techniques. Creating a "Wheel of Choice" (Nelsen, Lott & Glenn, 2000) is one way to visually represent the possible solutions to conflicts. Draw a large circle on a piece of posterboard. Divide the circle into sections. Label each section with a strategy for solving problems, such as

- ★ apologize,
- ★ walk away,
- ★ ignore it,
- ★ add it to the class meeting agenda,
- ★ count to ten to cool off,
- ★ use an I-message,
- ★ flip a coin,
- ★ shake hands and take turns, and
- ★ make another choice.

Post the wheel in an area that is easily accessible to children. Encourage them to "check the wheel" as needed.

Another way to help solve conflicts is to establish a "Decision-Making Box" in the classroom. In a small container, place a quarter (or two-sided counter) for flipping heads or tails, a number cube for rolling to determine who gets the highest number (to go "first"), and two straws of unequal length for drawing to see who gets the longer straw to get their way. In a class meeting, describe possible methods for making a decision. Enlist children's help in brainstorming other solutions. Place the box in an easily accessible location for anyone in the class to use.

STORY FROM A CHILD

Jorge, kindergarten

I always used to get into arguments with Jay, but now we do "Rock, Paper, Scissors" to decide. We made the rules for it and put it in this box the class uses. Then we do "Rock, Paper, Scissors" and we can check for sure if "paper covers rock." I don't argue anymore—I just do "Rock, Paper, Scissors."

STORY FROM A CHILD

John Michael, 1st grade

When I get mad, it is hard for me to think about doing the right thing. My brain knows not to push people, but sometimes I do. So, my teacher called a meeting with me and some of my friends. She asked us to think of how they could help me, and we thought up "Wheel." If they see me getting mad, they just say, "Wheel," and I walk over to the wheel. My friends help me.

Ms. Mozelle Duncan, kindergarten

By the third year I taught first grade, I was very proud of my ability to run an organized class. If children had problems, I could handle it without missing a beat. If two children were talking when I was teaching, I made both of them move and would not let them sit together for the rest of the day. If children were fighting over a toy, I decided which child deserved to play with the toy first and gave the toy to that child. If there was an argument in the home center, I simply closed that center for the day. If center time got too noisy, I ended center time and made all the children sit at their desks and do seat work. By the second month of school, children in my class were quiet and compliant. We really didn't have that many problems.

Then that summer I attended a workshop about conflict resolution among children. I was shocked. The presenters looked down on almost everything I thought I was doing so well. They said that when adults solve children's problems, they are robbing children of important learning. It took me a couple of days to realize that what they were saying was probably true. I changed my ways of looking at children's conflicts that next year, and I started teaching children how to solve their own problems. It was hard at first, but I am so glad I attended that workshop. The fourth year I taught was different. Young children can solve their own problems when you teach them how.

STORY FROM A FAMILY

My grandson is in one of those conflict-resolution classrooms. One night, I admit it, I was yelling at Carlos to get into the bathtub. He looked at me and said, "Grandpa, I don't like it when you speak to me so disrespectfully, so I'll tell you what we'll do. I'll go wait in my bedroom. When you can speak in a normal tone of voice, come find me." At first, I was shocked. How dare that little boy talk to his elders in that way? But then I realized that these were Carlos's teacher's words coming out of his mouth. Carlos was learning a good way to handle problems with other people—even me.

For Introducing Issues That Lead to Conflicts and How They Can Be Resolved

How to Be a Friend by Laurie Krasny Brown and Marc Brown (Little, Brown, 1998)
Written in easily understood language, the book presents situations about friendship and suggests language to use in each situation. The cartoonlike format helps children easily locate the speech bubbles that offer the language suggestions. Topics include who can be your friend, ways to be a friend, joining in the fun, feeling shy, and dealing with bosses and bullies.

. . . .

Simon's Hook: A Story About Teases and Put-Downs by Karen Gedig Burnett
(GR Publishing, 1999)
In this book about bullying, the author empowers victims of teasing and put-downs by having characters in the book respond to the teasing in several different ways: ignoring the person doing the teasing, walking away, avoiding situations, and so on.

. . . .

Oliver Button Is a Sissy by Tomie dePaola (Harcourt Brace, 1990)
Name-calling and teasing are the issues in this book about a boy who likes to do things that other boys call "girl" things, such as dancing, playing with paper dolls, and picking flowers. Even Oliver's father thinks he should do more "boy" things. However, people change their opinions when Oliver tap-dances in a talent show.

. . . .

Chrysanthemum by Kevin Henkes (Greenwillow, 1991)
Until Chrysanthemum started kindergarten, she believed her parents when they told her that her name was perfect. On the first day of school, the children in her class giggle when they learn her name. Chrysanthemum's music teacher—whose first name is Delphinium—and her loving parents help her learn to confront the taunting and to love her name again.

. . . .

Hooway for Wodney Wat by Helen Lester (Houghton Mifflin, 1999)
This book addresses making fun of a child with a disability—in this case, a speech impediment—and boasting and bullying. Since Wodney cannot pronounce the letter *r*, his classmates make jokes about it and tease him often.

Continued next page

Literature LINKS

Angel Child, Dragon Child by Mary Surat (Scholastic, 1989)
Ut's family moves from Vietnam to the United States. At school, Ut's classmates do not accept her because she looks different from them and dresses differently. Not only does Ut have to deal with the rejection of her peers, her mother is still in Vietnam and Ut misses her desperately. Eventually, children in the school come to see more similarities than differences between themselves and Ut, and they save money to send for Ut's mother.

Yoko by Rosemary Wells (Scholastic, 1998)
Other children make fun of Yoko when she brings her traditional Japanese lunch— sushi, rice rolls with cucumber, shrimp, seaweed, and tuna—to school. Realizing Yoko's predicament, Mrs. Jenkins, the teacher, plans International Food Day. Timothy, her new friend, eases her rejection into acceptance by the other children.

Crow Boy by Taro Yashima (Viking, 1955)
Crow Boy is singled out because he is different from the other children at the school. He is smaller than anyone and the other children call him "stupid" and "slowpoke." But after six years of school, a kind teacher recognizes and nurtures Crow Boy's knowledge of birds and nature. This recognition changes everyone's ideas about Crow Boy.

William's Doll by Charlotte Zolotow (HarperTrophy, 1972)
William wants a doll. His brother, the boy next door, and his father try to redirect his attention to basketball and an electric train. While he likes to play with those things, he still wants a doll. His grandmother intercedes on his behalf with wise words for his father.

As with other changes in behavior, it takes time and many reminders for children to understand and use the language you are teaching. Some days it may feel like you spent most of the time reminding children about appropriate language and supporting children in resolving conflicts. We still have days when we wonder if we are making any difference at all. But we always start the next day determined to teach and support the language that fosters a sense of community. Looking at the school year as a whole, we know that time spent early in the year helping children learn this skill is worth the investment. As the year progresses, you spend less and less time helping children resolve their conflicts because they gain the ability to solve them on their own.

Summary

Teaching children the language they need to handle different situations and providing opportunities for them to practice using it empower them to handle these situations on their own. They will know what to do at least most of the time, thus saving you time. When given appropriate learning opportunities, children know what to do when they need your attention, when they need something from a classmate, when they want to join a group of children, or when they have a conflict with another child.

Supporting Academic Learning

Academic lessons call for specialized teacher talk just as guiding children toward appropriate school behaviors does. Both kinds of teacher talk are equally important. Many times, teachers, even those who concentrate on using appropriate language to support children's social and emotional development, do not think about the language they use to support children's academic development. This chapter focuses on appropriate teacher talk to introduce topics of study, teach specific skills, teach specific content areas, respond to children's work, guide the work of individuals or small groups, challenge high-ability students, and support struggling students.

Introducing Topics of Study

There are no magic words for teachers to use when introducing new topics of study. The most important thing to remember is that the enthusiasm you show in the initial discussion sets the stage for children's interest in that topic. The enthusiasm you demonstrate when you initiate a conversation about a new topic is contagious—it spreads to most, if not all, children in the class, capturing their attention and pulling them into the topic.

Introducing Topics of Study

★ "Guess what? This morning there was a letter in my box that was addressed to you. Do you want me to read it to you?" (Ask the principal, another teacher, or an adult "friend" of the class to write a letter asking the class to research a particular topic and share that information with them. This motivates children by providing an audience and a reason for learning that extends beyond the classroom.)

★ "Last night, I went to _____ (the park, a museum, a bookstore, the library, or any other place that might have artifacts, specimens, or written material related to the topic being introduced), and guess what I saw!"

★ "You will not believe what I found last night. I could not wait to get to school to share this with you."

★ "You are not going to believe this, but I read (or saw on television or heard on the radio or was told by a friend) that _____ (introduce some obscure fact related to the topic being introduced, e.g., there are lizards that can run on top of water in a lake or slow-moving river). Can you believe that? Why don't we try to find out some more about _____ (topic)?"

★ "The kindergarten class down the hall has been studying _____ (topic being introduced). They have learned some pretty exciting things like _____ (mention some interesting facts related to the topic, e.g., bats sleep upside down, and they are mammals even though they fly like birds!). Do you think you would like to research _____ (repeat topic) and see if we can find out more facts like this?"

Most children are eagerly drawn into a topic when a teacher sits in front of her class with a bag in her lap, drops her voice to barely above a whisper, and announces, "You will not believe what I found last night. I could not wait to get to school to share this with you." Whether the object in the bag happens to be an artifact, a science specimen, or a book, children invariably want to know—right away—what it is and how it relates to them. This is where your acting skills come into play: waiting for momentum to build, pausing to add drama, widening eyes in exaggerated amazement, and bending over to carefully cradle the object. Suggested language for these situations is listed on page 103. No matter which introductory statement you use, delivering it in a dramatic tone of voice helps win children's attention.

Introducing a new topic to a class is one of those times that teachers can call upon their acting skills. Whether your tone of voice is that of whispered excitement or a louder, more passionate one, modeling enthusiasm for a new topic is important. The more excited you appear about this new topic of study, the more excited children tend to be. Modeling excitement and interest may not always convince young children that they want to learn this new concept, but it certainly goes a long way toward capturing their initial attention.

A Classroom Conversation

A Second-Grade Class Meeting

Mrs. Bills: [whispering] I need you to be very, very quiet this morning. I have something under this blanket that might be scared if we get noisy. When you are ready to listen to me whisper, look straight into my eyes. Okay, everyone is ready. I am going to give you some hints about what is under the blanket, and I want you to make predictions about what you think it is. Remember, predictions have to be based on something you know. Predictions are not wild guesses. Would "giraffe" be a good prediction?

Children: No-o-o-o.

Mrs. Bills: Why is that?

Jacob: 'Cause it's too little for a giraffe! Even a baby giraffe would be bigger.

Mrs. Bills: Good answer. Jacob used what he knew about the size of animals to reject "giraffe" as a good prediction. Okay, are you ready for the first clue? This animal is a mammal. What do you know about the thing that is under the blanket?

Mike:	It's warm-blooded.
Katherine:	It has hair on its body.
Katie:	Its mother fed it with milk from her own body.
Mrs. Bills:	You guys remembered three characteristics about mammals, so now you know that the thing under the blanket is warm-blooded, has hair on its body, and that its mother fed it with her own milk. Now, knowing those things, what are some good predictions for the thing under the blanket?
Samantha:	It's a puppy.
Mrs. Bills:	What do you guys think about Sam's prediction? Is it a good one? *[Writes "puppy" on a chart tablet]*
Children:	Yes!
Mrs. Bills:	Why?
Alex:	'Cause it could be a little puppy, so it's the right size, and dogs are warm-blooded, and have hair, and feed their babies.
Mrs. Bills:	Right! But is "puppy" the only good prediction you can think of?
Stephanie:	How about "kitten"?
Mrs. Bills:	Okay. . . *[Writes "kitten" on chart tablet]*
Max:	Or a horse. *[Mrs. Bills writes "horse" on chart tablet]*
Katherine:	No, a horse is too big.
Mrs. Bills:	I think Katherine is right. Even a colt would be bigger than what is under the blanket. *[Crosses off "horse"]* So far we have two good predictions: puppy and kitten. They both are the right size and they have the characteristics of mammals. Here is another clue. How does this information affect your predictions? The thing under the blanket has special teeth that keep growing its whole life.
Three children:	Hamster!
Mrs. Bills:	*[Writes "hamster" on chart tablet]* What a prediction! Why did you say "hamster"?

Carolyn:	'Cause our hamster has teeth like that. That's why we have to give him stuff to chew on so its teeth don't get too long.
Mrs. Bills:	That is certainly true. What does that information do to your other prediction? Could it be a puppy or a kitten?
Children:	No-o-o-o. *[Mrs. Bills crosses off "puppy" and "kitten"]*
Jacob:	Puppies and kittens don't have that kind of teeth, just rodents, so the animal under the blanket has to be a rodent and it has to be little, and a hamster is a rodent and it's sort of the right size, so it's a hamster.
Mrs. Bills:	You guys are getting so good at stating what you know to make a prediction. Everything Jacob just said is true, but the prediction is not true. So, put your thinking caps on and chat with a partner. See what you can come up with.

[Children talk among themselves.]

Mrs. Bills:	Okay, now I am ready to write more predictions. What did you come up with?
Various children:	Guinea pig, rat, gerbil, squirrel . . .
Mrs. Bills:	I can't believe how good these predictions are. Do you realize that you are listing just about all the rodents that you know? And one of your predictions is correct. Here's one more clue, the animal under the blanket has two names, not one.
Children:	Guinea pig.
Mrs. Bills:	Right! Now, I want you to tell me what you know about guinea pigs.

Mrs. Bills continues to transcribe what children say they know about guinea pigs and then leads them into listing questions related to what they want to learn about guinea pigs. This framework—focusing children on a new topic, connecting it to something they already know, drawing out of the class information related to the new topic, then eliciting questions about the topic—could be used to introduce almost any topic.

Drawing children into a topic is like acting on the stage. The presentation of the topic is what initially captures children's interest—and good teachers use any and all of the skills at their disposal to capture this attention. Likewise, when introducing skills, teachers also search for ways to capture children's interest.

Introducing Skills

When introducing a new skill to a class, you need to make sure that children know exactly why this skill is important and how they will use it. Otherwise, they tend to not pay attention.

Introducing a New Skill to Children

★ "Normally, teachers don't even think about teaching _____ (new skill) until third grade, but you guys are so smart that I think you are ready to learn _____ (the skill)."

★ "If you are going to keep up with all the cans donated to this year's Canned Food Drive, you need to know how to _____ (calculate running totals or add double-digit numbers). So pay attention."

★ "This is something that Eric Carle (or another favorite author) does all the time. I know that you guys want to be good authors, so let's look at some Eric Carle books to see how he uses _____ (the writing skill being introduced)."

★ "If you want to keep getting better at writing, _____ is something that you need to know so your audience can understand your writing better."

★ "Mathematicians use this strategy all the time. Listen carefully."

★ "Do you want to learn to do this? I know some shortcuts. Watch!"

★ "Some children have trouble learning to _____. It can be hard. But I can help you learn some ways to make it easier if you just look very carefully with me right now."

As with a new topic, the more excitement you can generate when introducing a new skill, the more interested children will be. Some statements to use to introduce a new skill to children are listed in the box on page 107.

Children are more likely to learn a particular skill when there is a real reason for learning it. If they need the skill to do something that they believe is important, then they work harder to master that skill and apply it to their current work. For example, children need to learn to add running numbers because that is a real-world skill needed in many different situations. Still, to young children who do not yet need to add in their day-to-day lives that seems like a weak reason. They cannot make the connection between adding running totals and their future needs. However, if children are involved in a project where they need a skill to do something they consider important, they are more likely to want to learn that skill. Sometimes you have to create a need for that skill. For example, keeping up with the number of cans and boxes of food they are collecting for a canned-food drive is usually important to children. In turn, learning to calculate running totals becomes important, so children are likely to learn this skill fairly quickly (assuming they have the necessary prerequisite skills).

STORY FROM A TEACHER

Mr. Trey Jordan, 1st grade

I remember being in third grade and learning about the business format for letter writing. I don't know why, but I can still see that textbook with a generic letter addressed to Mr. John Doe at the XYZ Company. I remember copying that letter three or four times because my teacher kept insisting that I had not used my "best" handwriting. Maybe that is why I remember this, the pain of copying and recopying. Here I am teaching the format of a business letter a full two years earlier than I learned it, yet my students are excited about learning this new skill. After a field trip to our local science museum, they had questions. I brought in some formal business letters that had been sent to me so they could see the format used in those letters and explained that "adults write letters this way." I told them that if museum directors and curators were going to take them seriously, they had to write their letters following this adult model. They were so serious in writing their letters. They checked the model letters several times, wanting to make sure that their letters were taken seriously. When children see a need for learning some skill, they learn it so much more quickly and remember it for much longer.

It is best to teach a skill just before children need to use it to do something important to them, but this may not always be possible. When it is not, it is up to you to explain why that particular skill will be important to them sometime in the future. It is not enough to simply say, "You will need this in second grade" (or whatever the next grade level may be). The explanation needs to be more specific than that. For example, children need to learn punctuation so that their writing can be read easily. When children have a real audience for their writing, they are likely to want to use proper punctuation so that the people they write for can read their writing with ease.

Supporting Children's Learning

Most of a teacher's day is spent teaching specific knowledge and skills and supporting children as they learn that knowledge and master those skills. Part of that teaching process is leading children into stating what they know or what they want to know, explaining their thought processes, and connecting new knowledge and skills to something that they already know. Discussions of teaching reading, writing, math, and science follow. For each one, some generic statements for leading children in this process are listed in boxes.

READING

Reading is not a single skill, but a combination of complex skills. The way you go about teaching these skills is very important. You must figure out what children know about reading and what they need to know to become more competent, more fluent readers. Teaching reading is done most effectively with small groups of children who have similar ability levels or one-on-one.

Building comprehension skills is an important part of learning to read. Sometimes children can read the words but do not understand what they mean. Children need help in focusing on the meaning of the text. Below are several suggested phrases for leading children as you work with them on decoding and comprehension skills.

Positive
TEACHER TALK

Supporting Learning About Reading

For Decoding:

★ "Go slowly. Watch the words carefully to see what letters are there."

★ "Look all the way to the end of the word."

★ "Let's look at that word more carefully."

★ "What are some of the strategies we've talked about that you might use to figure out what this word is?"

For Comprehension:

★ "Does this story remind you of _____ (something you've done before, any other stories, etc.)? How?"

★ "Would what you know about _____ be important here?"

★ "How does that relate to _____?"

★ "Try that again. Does that sentence make sense?"

★ "What have you done that is like what _____ (a main character) does? What have you done that is different from what _____ (a main character) does?"

★ "Does that seem reasonable?"

WRITING

Writing also combines a number of diverse skills. Supportive language from teachers is important to children's continuing progress in writing. Some of the language supports children as they move into more conventional forms of writing—correct spelling, correct punctuation, correct grammar, and so on. You need to acknowledge what a child knows and uses accurately, and point out one or two things that need to be worked on. Other supportive language focuses on revision, rewriting to make a piece of writing better: more detailed, more descriptive, clearer, and so on. Some of the generic statements you might use in supporting children's progress in writing are listed below:

Supporting Learning About Writing

★ "Listen to the word as I say it. (Repeat the word slowly.) What letter sound do you hear at the beginning of the word? Right now, just write the first letter and draw a line. We can come back to the rest of the word later."

★ "Where could you look to find out how to spell that word? Maybe in a book we've read? Maybe on our word wall? Maybe in a dictionary in the writing center?"

★ "Tell more about this part of your story. How could you add that information to your story?"

★ "Hmm, I wonder _____."

★ "What could you do to make that idea clearer to your reader?"

★ "Did you mean that the character _____ (acted in a certain way, had a particular feeling, etc.)? Then say it so the reader understands that."

★ "Listen to me read this sentence. (Read a weak sentence.) What other action word might make this sentence more interesting?"

★ "Listen to me read this sentence. (Read a weak sentence.) What word or two might create a stronger picture in your mind?"

★ "Could you add something to make this piece of writing paint a stronger picture in the mind of your readers?"

MATH

Teaching mathematical concepts to children is probably as much about ways you help them manipulate numbers and number concepts as it is about the words that you choose to use in your explanations. However, the language you use when teaching mathematics needs to be precise. Often, the teaching of mathematical concepts is best accompanied by appropriate manipulatives. After introducing the manipulative, describe the calculations or the problem-solving strategies in clear, concrete terms that young children can understand. Use language that helps children understand the concept and explain their thought processes as they work on different types of mathematical problems. Some supportive teacher language is listed below:

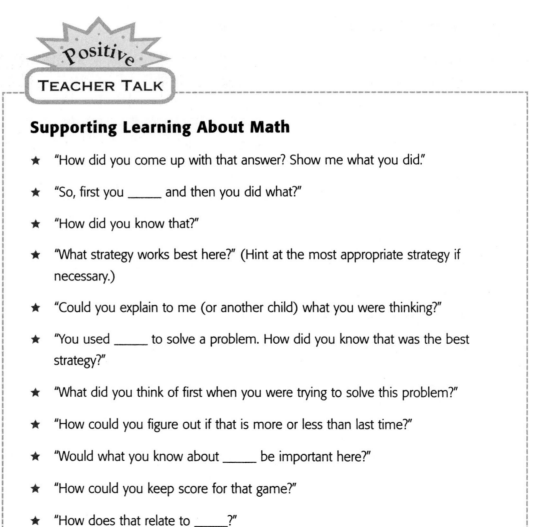

Positive TEACHER TALK

Supporting Learning About Math

★ "How did you come up with that answer? Show me what you did."

★ "So, first you _____ and then you did what?"

★ "How did you know that?"

★ "What strategy works best here?" (Hint at the most appropriate strategy if necessary.)

★ "Could you explain to me (or another child) what you were thinking?"

★ "You used _____ to solve a problem. How did you know that was the best strategy?"

★ "What did you think of first when you were trying to solve this problem?"

★ "How could you figure out if that is more or less than last time?"

★ "Would what you know about _____ be important here?"

★ "How could you keep score for that game?"

★ "How does that relate to _____?"

SCIENCE

Much like mathematics, science is a subject that children learn better when they are engaged in hands-on activities. In addition to the hands-on work, children need to learn to approximate the very precise language of scientists to describe their work. Teachers need to model this precision as they discuss science topics.

Supporting Learning About Science

★ "Scientists don't just look at something. They observe it very carefully. Let's observe _____ and see what details we can describe (draw, write about)."

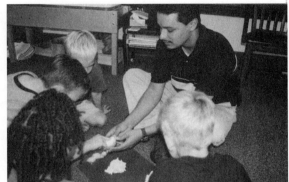

★ "Scientists say what they think will happen in an experiment. They call that predicting. Let's predict what will happen when _____."

★ "Where do you think we could find out more information about _____ (any science topic)?"

★ "Scientists know that they have to record their results very carefully. Let me show you a couple of ways to record your results."

★ "What does that remind you of?"

★ "Have we ever seen something like this before?"

★ "Would what you know about _____ be important here?"

★ "How does that relate to _____?"

★ "Do those _____ (leaves, tracks, bubbles, fossils, etc.) have a pattern? Why do you think that?"

★ "Has that ever happened before?"

Responding to Children's Work

The words that you use when responding to children's work are a major part of supporting children as they learn new knowledge and skills. Instead of glancing at a child's work and offering some generic phrase as acknowledgment, make careful language choices to respond much more specifically. View the moments when you respond to children's work as special teaching opportunities. In these moments, respond to one child about one specific piece of work. Very few papers created by young children are totally wonderful or totally awful. So, quickly examine the work and find something positive to say about it, as well as one thing that could be changed to make the work better.

In these brief comments, you reinforce both the knowledge and skills the child has mastered and those that the child has not yet mastered (or challenge a child to do something beyond what the work is showing or briefly teach a new concept). For example, for a kindergartner who is working on representational painting, you might respond to a watercolor rainbow by saying, "Jessica, you remembered the order of the colors of the rainbow: red, orange, yellow, green, blue, purple! I'll bet you were thinking about our rainbow song when you painted this. Maybe the next time you see a rainbow, take a closer look to see if it really just hangs in the sky or if both ends touch the ground."

STORY FROM A CHILD

Katie, 2nd grade

My old teacher just put a sticker on my papers. But my new teacher tells me what I did good on and what I can do better on. I like to make my work better and now I know how to do that.

Too many teachers fall into the habit of looking at children's work and making the comment "good job." This generic statement of adult acceptance is almost like white noise. "Good job" does not explain to the child exactly what it is about their work that is good or what he or she might do to improve the work. The comment "good job" undermines children's independence, their own pleasure in their work, and their

interest in it. It also interferes with how good a job children actually do when adult praise is not given.

In his article "Five Reasons to Stop Saying 'Good Job,'" Alfie Kohn (2001) suggests choosing one of the three following reactions to a child's work:

1. Say exactly what you see in their work;

2. Ask a question about their work; or

3. Simply say nothing.

You might comment, "You certainly worked hard on your story today," or "Look at the detail you used in your drawing this morning." Simple, evaluation-free statements let children know you are carefully examining their work and truly paying attention to what they are doing. Sometimes a probing question may be more appropriate, for example, "What was the hardest part of this picture for you to draw?" or "How did you figure out how to make this part the right size?" Questions like these also let children know that you are truly interested and paying close attention to their work.

Ms. Fayaka Dunbar, kindergarten

I've always heard the phrase "out of the mouth of babes," but the other day, I realized just how true that adage is. I was walking around my class, checking each child's work. In my mind, I was making sure that everyone understood the concept of ABB, ABB patterning. As I made a check mark on one child's paper, I heard a student comment to another child sitting beside him, "Don't worry if you mess up, she'll say 'good job' anyway." That comment really hit me. I did not realize that with every check mark I wrote came a "good job" comment. I thought about that comment all evening and finally vowed to never use that phrase again, to make specific comments about each child's work from the next day forward. Every now and then, I hear myself commenting "Good job" to a student. It's a hard habit to break, but I am working on it.

Guiding the Work of Individuals

Regardless of grade level, each year early childhood teachers need to explain very explicitly to children what working alone looks like in that classroom. Some teachers prefer that children do not help one another on individual work or even talk during these periods of time. Other teachers encourage children to ask a nearby classmate when they have a question about the work or need help completing it.

Positive
TEACHER TALK

Questions for Guiding the Work of Individuals

★ "Earlier this morning I asked you to _____. Are you doing it now?"

★ "What should you be doing during _____ (math practice time, etc.)?"

★ "If I saw you making good decisions during _____, what would I see?"

★ "I remember that we listed the behavior we wanted to see on that chart. Check it to see if you are doing the happy-face or sad-face things."

Whatever your preferences, communicate them very precisely—and provide children opportunities to practice those behaviors before holding children accountable for them. As with any new behavior, most children learn these preferences rather quickly, but some need extra time and support.

Challenging High-Ability Students

When working with high-ability students, as with any child, teachers need to choose words very carefully. Children who fall into the category of gifted and talented—whether or not they have been officially tested and labeled—need their teachers to identify their areas of strength and challenge them to think creatively and produce work at the level of their potential.

Most early childhood teachers have students with a wide range of ability levels. In trying to meet the needs of all children, teachers sometimes shortchange the higher-ability students. Knowing that the higher-performing students are working at or above grade level, many teachers subconsciously neglect them to spend more of their time teaching the lower-performing students.

Gifted and talented children need as much of your attention as any other group of children. Therefore, you need to think carefully about the language you use to support and challenge these children.

Positive

TEACHER TALK

Working With High-Ability Students

★ "Your answer is right. Now I want you to think about how you could explain how you arrived at this answer. Could you explain (or write) all the things you were thinking when you were solving this problem?"

★ "Well, what if we _____? Would we get the same results?"

★ "How could you make that _____? Would that change the way you got the answer?"

★ "What if you _____?"

Mrs. Woods was one of the best things that ever happened to our son, John Michael. Ever since he was a little boy, everyone has seen John Michael as a really smart boy. And he has been. But by second grade, he seemed to be getting the idea that he was the smartest little boy who ever lived. That was hard for us, because he actually was the smartest child in his classes in kindergarten and first grade, but he was getting so overly confident.

Then, in second grade, Mrs. Woods came into his life. It was obvious that she respected all children, but she didn't go easy on John Michael. She recognized how smart he was, but she didn't let him take over the class. She had private talks with him about letting other children have their turns at answering the questions she posed to the whole class and limited the number of times John Michael could answer those kinds of questions. Whenever he was finished with something she had asked the whole class to do, she didn't allow him to do whatever he wanted while other children caught up (like his other teachers did). She was right there with another task—another question for him to answer—and it was always something more complex, deeper than the original assignment. He wasn't asked to do more work because he was smart. She asked him to do more complicated work. She challenged him every day that he was in her class. Mrs. Woods really knew how to work with high-ability students.

Supporting Struggling Students

It is just as important to choose words carefully when working with children who are struggling learners. These children desperately need someone to believe in them and to teach them in ways that they learn best. There is no single right way to teach any concept. In many cases, children who come into our early childhood classes as struggling students are children who have not been taught in ways that they best understand. It is our responsibility to find the ways that our students learn best, and at the same time build their perceptions of themselves as learners. The best way to instill self-esteem in young children is to create learning experiences in which they are successful.

Some teachers use phrases that have the opposite effect from what they intend. A teacher trying to encourage a reluctant child to apply a new skill may say, "Oh, come on. Try this. It is easy." A child who does not find this particular skill easy concludes (in his mind) that he must be stupid. After all, his teacher said it was easy, so if he cannot do it, then it must be his fault. It is much better for a teacher to say to a struggling child, "I know this is hard to understand, but that is why I am here. We are going to work together to figure out the best way for you to learn this. That's what teachers are for."

Working With Struggling Students

★ "Of course you don't know this. That is why you are in first grade (or whatever grade level child is in). This is something that you are supposed to learn in first grade."

★ "It is my job to help you learn this. So, let's start here and . . ."

★ "I know this is not easy, but let's work together. I know that together we can figure out a way to help you remember _____."

★ "Look at this (a work sample from earlier in the year). Look at how much progress you've made already this year."

★ "Everyone is better at some things than others. You are great at _____. _____ (an area where the child struggles) is something that is not quite so easy for you, but we can work together and you will learn this."

★ "You have been working hard at _____ (area where child struggles). I can see that you are making progress, and I am proud of how hard you are working."

★ "I'm going to keep on helping you."

As with other situations in early childhood classrooms, it is sometimes helpful to use appropriate children's literature to launch a conversation with a child about something he or she is struggling with. Some of these books are listed on page 120.

Literature LINKS

For Children Who Struggle Academically or Who Have Low Self-Esteem

Pinduli by Janell Cannon (Harcourt Brace, 2004)
Pinduli's mother has always told her that she's the most beautiful hyena ever. But the other animals do not believe this. A case of mistaken identity allows Pinduli to do something great, changing the way she is viewed by all the animals. This story of self-acceptance and treating others with respect can be used to help children see themselves in a more positive light.

· ·

It's Hard to Be Five: Learning How to Work My Control Panel by Jamie Lee Curtis (Joanna Cotler Books, 2004)
Curtis uses a "control panel" as a great mechanism for young children to understand how they can "turn on" appropriate behaviors. This book could be used to encourage appropriate school behavior or harder work on areas in which children struggle.

· ·

The Crayon Box That Talked by Shane Derolf (Random House, 1997)
Derolf's simple poem reminds readers that when everyone works together, the world is more colorful and that everyone has an important role within his or her community.

· ·

Winners Never Quit by Mia Hamm (HarperCollins, 2004)
In one game, Mia quits playing soccer before the end of the game. She is afraid that her team will lose, so she quits before she loses. Mia's brothers and sisters do not let her play soccer with them anymore, and over time, Mia comes to the understanding that teamwork is more important that actually winning.

· ·

Leo, the Late Bloomer by Leo Lionni (HarperCollins, 1994)
Leo grows at his own pace, despite the fact that Leo's father is watching and waiting for his son to "bloom." Lionni makes it clear that it is perfectly fine for Leo to be who he is and to be working at his own level. This book could be used to encourage children who feel that they are behind others in their class.

Sammi Jo, 2ⁿᵈ grade

When I was in kindergarten and first grade, I thought I was dumb. There were lots of times I didn't understand things, but I pretended I did. I didn't want the other kids to know I was dumb. So I stayed real quiet, and my teachers kind of ignored me. My second-grade teacher is different. She thinks I am smart and she helps me. She tells me things again and shows me how to do things and I am doing lots better in school.

Ms. Gwendolyn Woods, 2ⁿᵈ grade

Every struggling student is different, but the one thing they have in common is the need to know that their teacher believes in them, their teacher believes they can, and will, learn whatever it is that they are struggling to learn.

Summary

The words that you use when teaching the whole class, small groups of students, or individuals have a powerful effect on children's learning. Your words can draw children into learning experiences and support their learning or put them off and hinder it.

Teaching Signals: Nonverbal Teacher Talk

Teachers who value the classroom community simply do not spend their time giving oral directions about behavior all day long. Of course, many children need reminders about certain behaviors. But these teachers support these children differently. They do not single out individual children for negative attention, embarrass a child, or cause the whole group to feel self-conscious. Teachers who strive to maintain a sense of community among children often use signals—visual, verbal, or even musical—to support children's self-control rather than constantly making statements about behavior (Kriete, 1999).

Consider this scenario: During a single read aloud in her kindergarten classroom, Mrs. Brown interspersed reading the text with several side comments, trying to correct children's behavior. She knew that a disruption from one child or a few children could put the whole lesson off track. She was doing what she thought was best. The read aloud lasted only 12 minutes, yet in that time Mrs. Brown gave nine verbal directions to individual students or to the whole group. She said:

1. "Sit down on your bottoms."

2. "Not everyone can see. Sit down."

3. "John Michael, keep your hands to yourself."

4. "I need all eyes on the book."

5. "Listen, everybody, listen."

6. "Sh-h-h-h-h-h."

7. "John Michael, hands . . . "

8. "I need everyone to look at the book."

9. "Sh-h-h-h-h-h."

Not only do directions such as these take an inordinate amount of time during the day, they also disrupt the learning. Imagine listening to a wonderful story interrupted every minute or so with statements such as "I've asked you all to sit down."

In this classroom, Mrs. Brown saw herself as the one who regulated all the behaviors in the class. Therefore, she found herself giving oral directions to children dozens of times a day. Most of those comments related to managing children's behavior or misbehavior: sit down, stand up, stop pushing, don't hit anyone, look at me, stop talking, etc. With no investment from children, these phrases worked only for the instant after they were expressed. There was almost no carryover to other similar situations.

Teachers who subscribe to this theory of correcting all of children's misbehaviors use such oral phrases all the time. They use them while they read aloud or give instructions about writing a letter or playing a game. Without really realizing what they are doing, teachers frequently stop the whole class's instruction to tell *one* child to either do something or stop doing something. These reminders interrupt the entire group and consume a lot of class time.

Teachers who value community in their classes and strive to support their students' self-control know that not all of the talking a teacher does is oral. Teacher talk also includes nonverbal signals or sounds, usually employed as children are making behavior choices. These signals are valuable tools for teachers of young children.

As with routines, signals should be explained and practiced before children are expected to successfully follow them (Bickart et al., 1999). Introduce and define signals using very concrete terms. Together with children, decide what signal to use and what it means. Then practice using it and evaluate its effectiveness, adapting and changing the procedure as necessary.

Using Visual Signals

Nonintrusive visual signals give directions without interrupting what is already happening in the classroom. Flicking the lights on and off has long been used as a visual signal to get children's attention. But this interrupts the work of the entire class, and, in some situations, that may not be necessary. Different types of visual signals are available for use. Some teachers create their own signals, while others use the signs of the American Sign Language and/or finger spelling. Also, the teacher and a particular child may establish their own, private signaling system.

STORY FROM A TEACHER

Ms. Susan Collins, 1st grade

I never realized how many times a day I shushed my class until a colleague videotaped one of my math lessons. We had planned to use the videotape as part of a presentation we were giving at a conference. My friend asked me if I realized that I was shushing the class quite a lot. When I watched the tape, I was both surprised and embarrassed. That little noise had become so much a part of me that I didn't even realize I was doing it almost every minute of my lesson. I talked to several other teachers and finally decided that I would try some sign language to signal students instead of telling them to stop talking, to look at me, or to listen to me. Maybe it was the novelty of the signals, but my students really responded to them. The next week we redid the videotape. The children's behavior didn't really change, but the feel of the lesson was much different. When I signaled instead of nagged, it was different. And when we showed the video during our presentation, we got more questions about the signals than the math lesson.

CREATING SIGNALS

The simplest signals to use are those that just seem to come naturally. Holding up your hand, palm facing out as a sign for stop, or an upraised index finger across your lips for quiet, or a crooked index finger gesture to come are all signals that teachers use almost unconsciously. Some teachers take this further, establishing signals with children in her classroom. A kindergarten teacher added a follow-up go signal to the stop signal. After signaling stop, she waved her hand to say, "Let's go." She used it as the class walked down the hall to the cafeteria, different classrooms, or the gym. After introducing signals to your class, you will find that children like to create their own signals. Some come and go within a week. Others are incorporated into the signal menu of your class.

SIGNING SIGNALS

American Sign Language, which consists of hand signs for each word or idea, is now the fourth most often-used language in the United States (Flodin, 1994). Using these signs as visual signals serves two purposes. First, you are supporting children's appropriate behavior with silent reminders. Second, you are teaching children usable words and phrases in a different language. Perhaps the easiest signs to incorporate in the classroom are the ones for "yes" and "no." "Yes" is indicated by shaking a closed fist up and down, and "no" is signed by tapping the index and middle fingers against the opposing thumb.

Yes

In the kindergarten class's read aloud mentioned at the beginning of this chapter, Mrs. Brown used nine phrases as she attempted to change children's behaviors. Some simple American Sign Language signs could have easily replaced her verbal directions. Instead of saying, "Sit down on your bottoms," she could have used the sign-language gesture for "be seated." This sign is made by holding out two fingers on the left hand, palm down, placing two fingers on the right hand, palm down, on top of the left-hand fingers, and moving both hands down slightly. The same signal could have been used when Mrs. Brown said, "Not everyone can see. Sit down."

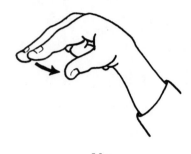

No

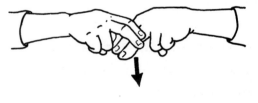

Sit

Announcing, "John Michael, keep your hands to yourself," not only disturbed the flow of the story, it also called everyone's attention to John Michael and his misbehavior. Even if it was for only a few seconds, the children's attention was directed away from what was happening in the story. Mrs. Brown could have made eye contact with John Michael and given the sign for "disturb" or "meddle" and shaken her head at the same time. This less-intrusive method would still have achieved the desired outcome—refocusing John Michael's attention on the task at hand.

My daughter's teacher uses many different signals to communicate with the children. I've spent enough time in the classroom to know most of the signals. I know the most serious one is when someone turns off the lights and announces, "Emergency group meeting." That means a problem has happened that everyone needs to help solve. Imagine our chagrin, when one night my husband and I were having a disagreement, our daughter walked into our bedroom, turned off the lights, and said, "Emergency group meeting, in my bedroom." My husband and I looked at each other for a moment, then walked into our daughter's bedroom. We had our emergency meeting and agreed that we would not fight so loudly anymore.

The sign that asks people to look at something is produced by making a "V" with the right hand, with the fingers pointing first at the eyes, then in the direction of what the person should look at. So, instead of saying, "I need all eyes on the book," Mrs. Brown could have made this sign then touched the book.

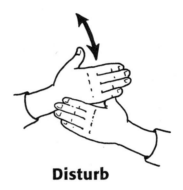

Disturb

Repeatedly asking children to listen to the story or shushing them becomes like white noise. After a while, children simply do not respond, or worse, they all join in, so that everyone is shushing and no one is actually being quiet. Instead of shushing the entire class or reminding children to "listen, everybody, listen," the teacher can communicate the request with the sign for "listen." Creating the "listen" sign in American Sign Language is almost instinctive—it is made by cupping the right hand, placing it behind the right ear, and turning the head slightly to the left. Instead of making many of her comments, Mrs. Brown could have signed "listen."

Listen

Literature LINKS

Resource Books About Sign Language

Handtalk by Remy Charlip, Mary Beth Miller, and George Ancona
(Macmillan, 1974)
Each page in this children's book shows a different letter, the sign for a word that begins with that letter, and photographs of a hand spelling out that word. Ancona's time-lapse photography enhances the explanation of the signs. Additionally, the fly pages in the front of this book have photographs to illustrate all the finger-spelling signals and the back pages have illustrations of some common signs.

. . . .

Handtalk Birthday by Remy Charlip, Mary Beth Miller, and George Ancona
(Macmillan, 1984)
In this sequel to *Handtalk*, Charlip takes both sign language and finger spelling another step. The text and signs describe the events of a birthday, and Ancona's clear photographs make the finger spelling and signing seem simple and accessible.

. . . .

The Handmade Alphabet by Laura Rankin (Puffin, 1996)
The illustrations in this book are detailed and realistically portray hands of different ages, sexes, and colors. The hands demonstrate the positions for the manual alphabet used in finger spelling. In addition to a hand showing how to make the letter, each letter shows an object, for example, the pointing finger for *I* points toward an icicle; *T* shows three thimbles and thread; and *X* is shown on an X ray.

FINGER-SPELLING SIGNALS

Finger spelling, in which words are formed letter by letter with the fingers of one hand, is a technique we use often. Rather than spell entire words, we tend to use the first letter of a word as a signal in the classroom. The sign for the letter *r* is made with the middle finger crossed over the index finger with the other fingers and thumb closed. When that letter is waved twice it becomes the signal that means "I need to use the restroom." The sign for *w* is three raised fingers, and is used for "I'm going to get a drink of water." The *l* sign (thumb extended and index finger raised) can mean "listen."

USING SIGNALS FROM THE REAL WORLD

Sometimes we use signals that children learn in situations outside school. Children involved in sports are familiar with the way coaches, referees, and umpires use silent signals to communicate with players. A baseball umpire signals that a player is safe or out. A classroom teacher could use those

Out

signals to indicate that a child should move (out) or that it is okay to stay where he is (safe). We involve our students in suggesting appropriate sports signals for communicating in the classroom. Many

Safe

children will be eager to add a signal from their experiences for class use. This is just one more small way to help children view the classroom as theirs.

Signals used in other real-world situations can be transferred into classroom use. Police officers control traffic with hand signals for when to stop, when to go straight, and when turns are allowed. Many workplaces are just too loud for verbal communication, so workers must use signals to communicate. Ground crews signal airline pilots as they pull away from the gate. Oil-rig workers signal one another. Crane

---

STORY FROM A TEACHER

Mr. Trey Jordan, 1st grade

I had five boys in my class who started taking tae kwon do lessons within a couple of weeks of each other. They became obsessed with it. Rather than ban tae kwon do from the classroom, I incorporated it into one of our routines. I asked the boys to teach the rest of the class the three phrases/actions they performed at the beginning and at the end of each lesson. The routine was shouting, "*sohgi,*" and standing very straight with legs slightly apart, hands pulled into fists, and arms bent so that the hands are placed at the top of the legs. Next, the children shouted, "*charyeot,*" brought their feet together and moved their arms down so that their palms touched their thighs. The routine ended with a quieter "*joobi,*" and a bow to the instructor. We used this signal when I needed to get the attention of the whole class. It felt a little militaristic to me, but the influence of tae kwon do was already in the classroom. This way I took something that was a potential problem and turned it into something that helped bring order to the group and helped children begin to recognize the discipline of tae kwon do.

operators typically cannot see what they are picking up or putting down, so they rely on other construction workers' signals to direct them. Any of these signals could be brought into the classroom, but it is very important that each new signal is properly introduced, explained, and practiced.

The entire class must understand what each signal means. One explanation and one practice session is usually not sufficient for all children in the group to understand. Someone may be absent on the day you explain a new signal, some children may not be paying attention, or a child may simply not understand it. A signal that is not understood by everyone can cause real confusion in the classroom.

STORY FROM A TEACHER

Ms. Wendy Chen, kindergarten

I have a friend who is a cameraman for a local television news program, so I was familiar with a floor manager's signals. One I introduced in my class was the "countdown to action" signal. In this signal, the floor manager holds up his hand with five fingers open and shouts, "5." Then he pulls in his thumb and shouts, "4." He proceeds, hiding one finger at a time as he shouts, "3, 2." When he gets to "1," he says nothing, but points his index finger toward whoever was on camera. That means that all the equipment is turned on and the show is live. That worked in my class for coming to the group meeting area or wrap-up of pair sharing. It worked well for this class, so I decided to talk about my friend again.

I explained to my class that the floor manager was also responsible for making sure the show went to commercials on time and ended on time. The signal he used to tell the anchor people to stop talking was to run his hand across his throat. That meant "cut." I made sure everyone understood the signal and we practiced. I thought this was a great signal for the class. Well, I thought that until one day when I overhead Marques tell another child that he was going to "cut you off at the neck." I was astonished. It had been weeks since anyone in the class had threatened another child. When I confronted Marques about his threat, he responded, "You do it all the time!" Shocked, I asked, "When have I ever said, 'I am going to cut you off at the neck'—to anybody? Marques responded, "You don't say it. You do this," and ran his hand across his neck. I couldn't believe it. For two weeks, this child thought I had been threatening children in the class. It made me realize again that young children are very concrete people and that I have to be careful in my communication with them.

CREATING PRIVATE SIGNALS BETWEEN THE TEACHER AND ONE CHILD

Some children need more support in their efforts to maintain self-control than other children. Every class has one or two children who fall into this category. In some classes, those children stand out. Visitors know the names of those children within the first few minutes of observing. Teachers tire of always standing up from wherever they are, walking over to the same child, and repeating the same conversation. The teacher may be reminding a child to use appropriate language, not to take things from other people, or just to use a quiet voice inside. After a few days, some teachers react to a child's repeated misbehavior by saying the child's name loud enough so that he or she can hear above the hum of the class and adding a word or two, such as, "Whitney—language," "Justin—don't grab," or "Maria—quiet."

Private signals between the teacher and child are much better than calling across the room. These private, visual signals can be very effective but, of course, they only work when the child is looking at the person giving the signal. So, be sure to catch a misbehaving child's eye before making the signal.

A Classroom Conversation

A Conversation With a First-Grade Child About Private Signals

Mrs. Clark:	Robert, it seems to me that you are having a bit of trouble with talking during group times. Is that true?
Robert:	I don't talk all the time.
Mrs. Clark:	That is true. You are not talking all the time, but you are talking enough that it is bothering other people. Remember yesterday when Shaundra told you to be quiet when I was reading *Strega Nona*?
Robert:	Yeah.
Mrs. Clark:	And during the same story time, didn't Shawn tell you not to try to talk like Big Anthony?
Robert:	Yeah.
Mrs. Clark:	Well, I think if two people have to tell you not to talk during one story time, that is too much talking.

Robert:	Okay.
Mrs. Clark:	Robert, I understand that it is hard to keep quiet if your brain thinks of something you want to say. I know that. But I can't let you disturb other children because they want to hear all of the story. I think you can understand that, right?
Robert:	Yeah.
Mrs. Clark:	I think maybe I can help you remember to let everyone hear all of the story. Would it be okay with you if we came up with an agreement on a way that I can help you remember?
Robert:	Yeah.
Mrs. Clark:	How about this? For the next few days, I need you to sit right in front of me when we have whole-group meetings. Let me show you where that is. Let's go over there *[leads Robert to group meeting area and sits in small chair where she sits during story times]*. Robert, you need to sit right here *[points to area of the floor right beside her]*. Good, that's right where you need to sit. Now, if you start to say something to another child during story time, I will move my foot and touch your foot with it. That way, it will be like me reminding you not to interrupt story time, and no one will see it. This signal is just between you and me, okay?
Robert:	Okay.
Mrs. Clark:	Let's practice. I'll pretend to read and you start to say something to a pretend person sitting beside you.
Robert:	I li— *[Mrs. Clark touches Robert's foot]*.
Mrs. Clark:	Great. You stopped talking as soon as I reminded you with our signal. Now, tell me what our signal is so I know that you know for sure what it is.
Robert:	I stop talking when your foot touches my foot.
Mrs. Clark:	And for that to happen, you need to sit right here, okay?
Robert:	Okay.
Mrs. Clark:	Robert, I think this is going to work. Let's try it for a couple of days and then meet again to check to see how it is working for you. Let's keep working together.

Katherine, beginning of 1st grade

Michael doesn't always look at the teacher, but I do. When Mrs. Woods is trying to give Michael a signal, I lean over and whisper, "She's looking at you." Nobody told me to do that. I just do. Michael needs my help.

Robert, end of kindergarten

When I went to my new school, I wasn't supposed to talk when the teacher was reading, but I did. We had a meeting. She told me she could help me remember not to talk. We talked about a private signal. I would sit by her. When I would start to talk, she would touch my foot with her foot. I learned not to talk. Then she didn't have to do that foot thing anymore.

Children who repeat undesirable behaviors or continually disrupt the flow of the class present another opportunity to use signals. When the child first misbehaves, you can signal "one." When the behavior is repeated, signal "two." Sometimes a young child is not aware of how many times he or she repeats a misbehavior. You and the child can agree with the number of "chances" he or she can get before a consequence occurs, or a goal can be set—"Now let me understand, Emmett, you are going to use self-control today and need only three reminders from me. Right?"

Using Auditory Signals

Of course, there are school situations in which all of the children should focus their attention on you at the same time. In these situations, a silent signal usually does not work. The signals that airline ground crews and construction workers use are effective only because everyone knows when someone will be signaling them, so they watch one another. Noisy times in schools are not times when children are looking at the teacher for signals. The cafeteria and the playground tend to be noisier than the classroom, so in these situations we often use signals that can be heard.

Many early childhood educators use a form of clapping as a signal. In our classrooms, we use a pattern of two claps, followed by three fast claps as a signal to stop whatever children are doing and look at us. We do not expect children to join in the clapping, and we strive to clap only one pattern before all children are looking. Once again, this takes practice on the part of both children and teacher. We introduce this signal by discussing times when we need the class's attention and need it quickly. These times include an emergency (paint is spilled and the class needs to be made aware of it quickly before someone steps in it), a celebration (three children working in the block center have completed the tallest tower ever built by the class), or a quick direction ("Sorry everyone, we've got to go to lunch right now. We'll finish this when we get back."). We practice this behavior with children. Children pretend to be working at their places and we pretend to be helping one child. Then one of us looks at the clock and says, "Oh my!" then claps in the pattern. Children practice zooming their eyes to us and listening for the directions.

The "countdown to action" signal is another audible signal. The teacher explains the desired behavior (pick up the scraps off the floor, straighten your folders on your table, put the books away, come to the group area, etc.) then begins a slow countdown—"5 . . . 4 . . . 3 . . . 2 . . . 1 . . . action!" This gives children an opportunity to judge how much time they need to complete the task and get to the indicated area.

Using Musical Signals

Many early childhood teachers use singing as a signal for changing activities. Almost all teachers of young children have launched into the song "Clean up, clean up / Everybody, everywhere / Clean up, clean up" to accompany the end-of-the-day cleanup time. Other teachers adapt familiar songs to the task at hand, like "This is the way we go to lunch / Go to lunch, go to lunch / This is the way we go to lunch / Having a good day" or "I've been cleaning up the classroom / All the live-long day / I've been cleaning up the classroom / Putting the trash away / Don't you hear the children singing / Let's get this job done / I've been cleaning up the classroom / And now it's done."

Teachers fortunate enough to have a piano in their classroom play a few measures of music to signal different activities. One kindergarten teacher plays the melody for the song that Carol Burnett used to end one of her television shows (". . . it's time to say so long . . .") to give her students a five-minute warning for cleanup. She plays the first

line of "The Ants Go Marching" to ask the children to line up at the door. Other teachers use electronic keyboards for these signals. Using the prerecorded rhythms to indicate the task or playing a short melody can become the class's signals.

STORY FROM A TEACHER

Ms. Nancy Lott, 2nd grade

I used to rely on flicking the lights on and off when I wanted the children's attention. That meant that I had to walk to the door where the light switch was located. Now I use a variety of musical signals. I keep a tone wand (a twisted and bent piece of aluminum wire that produces a vibrating, musical tone when tapped) by my desk, a thunder tube (a cylindrical tube with drum skin paper covering one end and a long coiled wire attached that, when shook, sounds just like a lightning and thunderstorm) on top of the filing cabinet, and a cricket snapper (the small, bent metal toy that produces a clicking sound) on the easel in the group area. No matter where I am in the room, some sort of musical signal is nearby.

Summary

A community of learners often develops shared signals to indicate behaviors desired by the group. These signals can be visual, using American Sign Language or finger-spelling techniques, or auditory, with teacher and children developing their own techniques or adapting ones from the real world. Musical tones and signals can also be used.

CHAPTER

8

Supporting Children
Who Experience Difficulty Being
Part of the Class Community

A colleague stopped by to visit with Tara, a veteran teacher of 27 years, about her first week of kindergarten. "How was it?" she inquired. Tara replied, "Oh, the children are coming together. I only have about two children who are not quickly fitting into our routine." They smiled in agreement—having only two such children was not bad at all.

138

At the beginning of the school year, most early childhood classes have a few children who experience some difficulty becoming part of the class's community. These children have different kinds of difficulties for various reasons. Some of them are not accepted easily as a part of the community because of challenging behaviors that push their peers—and even adults—away from them. They may be overly aggressive, have a great need to boss other children, constantly vie for adult attention, or exhibit other challenging behaviors. On the other hand, other children lack the appropriate social skills to interact successfully with their classmates or have emotional challenges that cause them to withdraw from the group. Whatever the issue, all of these children desperately need help and support from their teachers to overcome their challenges and become an integral part of a class community.

All children have the fundamental need to be a part of a group. They need a sense of belonging. However, by the time young children enter early childhood classes, some have developed particular behaviors that make it difficult for them to become part of the class community. Many factors contribute to the development of these behaviors. Most of them can be placed into one of two broad categories: biological risk factors (temperament, attention deficit disorder, complications of pregnancy and birth, malnutrition, language and cognitive disorders, even gender) or environmental risk factors (family factors and parenting styles, poverty and the conditions surrounding it, exposure to violence, turbulent times, violent media, negative child-care experiences) (Kaiser & Rasminsky, 2003).

Children who have one risk factor in their lives are no more likely to develop challenging behaviors than a child who has none. However, when a child has two such factors, they face a risk four times as great as the child who has none (Rutter, 2000). No matter which risk factors contribute to a child's difficulties, good teachers recognize that they have to address the child's real needs before they can begin helping the child change his or her behaviors, which, by now, are strongly ingrained. When you can identify why a child behaves in certain ways, then it is easier to determine how to meet that child's needs and to support the child in modifying behaviors.

Whether children have challenging behaviors or limited social skills, they need adults to work with them, to explicitly teach the more appropriate behaviors, and to encourage them as they work to change their inappropriate behaviors. At first, this may consume a significant amount of time. Some teachers struggle with spending time on activities that take away from academic time. However, when you take the time necessary to help children develop appropriate school behavior, you create a class in which more academic learning can occur. Just as important, you are helping children develop skills and characteristics integral to their successful school careers—and their adult lives.

Challenging Behaviors

Challenging behavior is any behavior that "interferes with children's learning, development, and success at play; is harmful to the child, other children, or adults; or puts a child at high risk for later social problems or school failure (Kaiser & Rasminsky, 2003). These behaviors are just as challenging to the child who exhibits them as they are to teachers and peers, but the child rarely knows how to go about changing them. The child needs adults to support him as he works through this type of change.

Many types of challenging behaviors are common to young children. Some children are aggressive toward others—usually toward other children but sometimes also toward adults. Some children have a strong need for power over their own lives and other people. They need to control people around them. Some children demand an unusually large amount of attention from adults. While these are the most common challenging behaviors, there are certainly others.

CHILDREN WHO ARE AGGRESSIVE

Many young children enter early childhood classrooms with few positive experiences related to being part of a group. Many have learned (from siblings or aggressive children in group-care settings) that hitting and pushing are ways to get what they want. These aggressive behaviors have been successful for them in the past and are not easy to change. However, aggressive behaviors must be stopped. A teacher cannot allow one child to hurt other children. Furthermore, classmates often reject aggressive children, and this rejection only makes the child's issues worse. Most aggressive children desperately want to belong to the group but do not understand how to do that.

There are two basic categories of aggression: direct and indirect. Each calls for a different response from the teacher. Some children get what they want by being physically aggressive. Other young children are simply impulsive, hitting, kicking, pinching, or biting when angry. These are direct forms of aggressive behavior. Indirect aggressive behaviors include bullying, teasing, ignoring rules, defying adult instructions, spreading rumors about peers, excluding peers, name-calling, and destroying classroom supplies and materials. Whether the aggression is direct or indirect, these children desperately need help from adults to learn how to behave more appropriately.

One component of supporting an aggressive child is preventing acts of aggression before they occur. When an adult knows a child very well, often the adult can "see" anger (or other negative emotions) building before the outburst occurs. When you observe a child in this anxious state, there are several ways to help the child calm down:

★ Gently ask the child, "Do you want to sit with me for a while?" or "Can I help?"

★ Ask open-ended questions to give the child an opportunity to tell his or her story and possibly regain a sense of control over whatever he or she is upset about, e.g., "Why don't you tell me how you are feeling?"

★ Validate the child's feelings by using active-listening statements, e.g., "I hear you saying that you are not happy that Marcia does not want to play with you. That makes you sad, right?"

★ Help the child see the problem in a more positive light, e.g., "You're learning something new. Making mistakes is how we learn." (Kaiser & Rasminsky, 2003)

Your body language and tone of voice are very important in these situations. An adult can actually lead a child into a calmer state by matching the child's tone of voice and body position, then slowly changing the tone of voice to more normal tones and position of arms, legs, and other body parts to less aggressive stances. In interactions such as this, many children will unconsciously mirror the adult model.

While preventing aggressive actions is desirable, it is not always possible. Early childhood classes are very hectic places, and a single teacher cannot always recognize the warning signs, so having strategies in mind to implement when aggressive acts occur in the classroom is important. Those strategies include:

★ Creating a calm, peaceful place in the classroom where a child who has hurt another child can go to calm down. This is often referred to as a "time-out," but the child should not be sent to this place as punishment. Instead, this calming place should give the child an opportunity to regain control, to teach him or her the strategy of getting away from the group when negative emotions are building, and to allow the rest of the class to continue with their activities. You might say, "Grady, I can see that you are really upset over having to share the blocks. Please go to the thinking chairs, and I'll be there in a minute."

★ Bringing the child close to you. Sometimes the close physical proximity of the teacher is enough to prevent a child from acting aggressively. You may simply move to the child or say, "Zachary, here's a spot on the rug where you can see better. Move over here by me."

★ Helping the child choose a place in the classroom where he or she can calm down (e.g., the listening center, where the child could listen to a favorite book or some kind of peaceful music, or the sand center, where the mere action of pushing one's hands through the sand calms some children). You might say, "I can see that you are upset. Go use the play-dough center and I'll come talk to you later."

No single strategy always works best, so you need to get to know individual children well and choose the strategy that best supports that individual child. While some children feel calmer when they are separated from other children and engaged in some kind of calming activity, others calm down more quickly when they are very close to a trusted adult. When working with an aggressive child, you need to try each one of the three strategies mentioned above to determine which one best supports that child.

Positive TEACHER TALK

Supportive Language for Aggressive Children

★ "It is my job to make this room a safe place to be. I will not let you hurt anyone in this class, and I will not let anyone hurt you."

★ "People are not for hitting."

★ "Jorge is not for hurting, just like you are not for hurting."

★ "I know you are going to have a self-controlled day. Today, if you find yourself getting angry, you are going to tell me or tell the person you are mad at. You are not going to hit or push anyone. Right?"

★ "Sam is not for pushing. How about you try saying, 'Excuse me. I need to walk through this center'? Then we can talk about how those words work."

A Classroom Conversation

A Conflict-Resolution Meeting With a Teacher and Two Students

Mrs. Johnson:	Mark and John Michael, we are here to talk about what happened this morning during center time. I am not sure how the problem started, but I do know that you both hit each other, and . . .
Mark:	He hit me first.
Mrs. Johnson:	We are not going to blame anyone, but it is my job to keep everyone in this class safe. I cannot let either one of you hit anyone else ever again.
John Michael:	But he hit me first.
Mrs. Johnson:	Again, let me say, we are not going to blame anyone. We need to figure out what you two can do when you are angry with someone instead of hitting them.

Mark:	But he took my marker. I was using that marker and he snatched it off my table.
John Michael:	You were not using that gray marker. It was just sitting there and you were coloring with the blue marker.
Mark:	I was gonna use it.
Mrs. Johnson:	Okay, let's start right there. John Michael, are you saying that you saw a gray marker on the table beside Mark, and you wanted to use the marker?
John Michael:	Yeah.
Mark:	But he just grabbed it.
Mrs. Johnson:	And that is not the way we do things in this class. John Michael, do you understand that Mark was upset when you took the marker?
John Michael:	*[shrugs]*
Mrs. Johnson:	Mark, you need to tell John Michael how you feel.
Mark:	*[just looks down at the floor]*
Mrs. Johnson:	Mark, say, "When you took the gray marker, it made me mad because I was going to use it in just a minute."
Mark:	When you took the gray marker, it made me mad because I was about to use it.
Mrs. Johnson:	Okay, John Michael, do you understand how Mark felt?
John Michael:	*[nods]*
Mrs. Johnson:	Mark, do you understand how John Michael felt when you hit him?
Mark:	Yeah.
Mrs. Johnson:	John Michael, please tell Mark anyway. Tell him that you did not like it when he hit you.
John Michael:	I do not like it when you hit me.
Mark:	Sorry.

Mrs. Johnson:	Mark, I am glad that you apologized to John Michael. That is one way we let other people know that we are sorry that we made a bad decision. But, it is important that we figure out what you guys are going to do the next time this happens.
John Michael:	I should ask, "Please, can I use the gray marker?" *[mimicking words he has heard in a recent class meeting]*
Mrs. Johnson:	Good, that would be using self-control. Mark, if John Michael said those words to you, would you have let him use the marker?
Mark:	When I was through with it.
Mrs. Johnson:	Okay, what words could you have used if John Michael said to you, "Please, can I use the gray marker?"
Mark:	I could say, "In a minute."
Mrs. Johnson:	John Michael, would you have been willing to wait until Mark was finished with the marker?
John Michael:	Yep.
Mrs. Johnson:	See guys, if you use words so that other people know what you want, this avoids hitting. Let's practice what you just agreed to. Let's go back over to Mark's table and both of you use the words you said you would use instead of hitting.

[The boys role-play the appropriate language.]

Mrs. Johnson:	That's great. You both used language to let each other know what you wanted, and neither one of you got angry this time. I am going to be listening for this kind of language from you in the next few days. I am proud of you both for solving this problem.

Ms. Deborah Diffily, kindergarten

At the end of the first day of school, every teacher in the building knew who Matthew was. He was not a child who was easy to miss. Matthew did everything a child can do on the first day of school to attract adults' attention. He hit and kicked other children, ran from the classroom (down the hall, out the door, and almost to the street before I caught him), cried (loudly), and screamed obscenities at the top of his lungs. On top of being a challenge in his behavior, Matthew was developmentally delayed. At 5 years old, he was more like a toddler. He was not used to being in a situation with other children, and he was not accustomed to doing anything he did not want to do. He did not play with other children at all. His language was at the stage of telegraphic speech, two-word phrases. Matthew was going to be a challenge. At the end of that first day, when almost every teacher in the school found me to ask about my new student Matthew, I kept wondering, "How am I going to help him become part of our class community?" And beyond that, "How am I going to get the other children in the class to want Matthew to be part of their community?" That year was a real challenge.

I had to work on Matthew's inappropriate behaviors one at a time. It was a slow process—getting him to sit quietly during our shared story times and other group situations, helping him understand how to play with classmates, shepherding him in learning to form and maintain friendships. He had to learn virtually all of the behaviors that would make him be accepted by other children. On the other end of the problem, I had to work with the other students—helping them understand why Matthew acted the way he did, trying to get them to understand that they, too, had a role in helping Matthew learn appropriate school behavior. But, over time, Matthew did make changes and the other children became more accepting of him.

By December, both Matthew and the other children in the class had made enough changes that our "wild child" had become an integral part of the class community. Matthew felt like he had friends, and the other children truly missed Matthew when he was absent. I find myself thinking of Matthew often when I see a child who is not really part of a class community. If Matthew can become part of a class community, I think any child can—with help and support from his teacher.

CHILDREN WHO NEED TO BE THE BOSS

Some young children have an unusually strong need for power (Nelsen et al., 2000). These children need to control their own lives, usually by taking the stand that they "do not have to do what other people tell them to do." And many of these children extend this need for power to include classmates. They want to tell other children what to do, how to do it, and when to do whatever it is the child is trying to control.

Adults can use multiple strategies with children who have a misguided need for power. One of the most effective strategies is redirecting the child toward positive power by asking the child for help with a particular task. When the child is in this state, do not fight or argue with the child. Simply withdraw from any conflict and offer the child some choices. Acting firmly and kindly, offer the child a limited number of true choices. Carefully avoid the lack-of-choice options that are sometimes used, e.g., "You can either do your work now or do it during recess." The limited options should be real options. Then, once the child has selected one, follow through to ensure the child actually completes the chosen option without giving in to the child or his need for control.

Positive
TEACHER TALK

Supportive Language for Children Who Need to Be the Boss

★ "I see that you really like to be in charge. Right now it is time for _____, and we must do _____."

★ "I see that you like to be in charge. Would you like to be in charge of _____?" (Offer the child two choices of a class task.)

★ "Please do not tell other children what to do. You are in charge only of yourself."

★ "You have many choices in this classroom, but you do not have a choice about _____ (whatever the issue is)."

★ "This is something you must do. What can I do to help you _____?"

Mr. Jonathan Lintz, kindergarten

There are always a few children who tend to boss other children around. Sometimes they are only children, accustomed to having things their way, or they have been in child-care settings in which they were the older child and became used to telling other children what to do. Some children just seem to be born with some characteristic that makes them emerge as leaders, telling peers what to do. I've had lots of children like that in my classes over the past few years, but this year's class was so different. By the end of the first week of school, I identified 18 out of 23 students as "bosses," some bossier than others. That's 18 children who wanted things their way. We have had class meeting after class meeting about how to treat other people. I've had lots of individual discussions this year about respecting our friends and not telling other people what to do. I've tried to redirect their desire to be in control of others by having them be in control of certain jobs in the classroom. I've come up with jobs for every child to be in charge of something every day. It's been a real challenge, but now that we are two months into the school year, I am finally beginning to see changes in the class. Children are finally beginning to treat one another in ways that I expect.

CHILDREN WHO CONSTANTLY VIE FOR ADULT ATTENTION

Some children demand more attention than other children. They constantly seek undue attention (Nelsen et al., 2000) throughout the school day. Although this behavior affects other children in the classroom, and they may become annoyed with such students, this behavior most annoys teachers. They also find themselves feeling irritated, worried, and sometimes even guilty. They typically react to attention-getting behaviors by reminding children about what they are supposed to be doing, coaxing children into appropriate behaviors, even doing things for children that they could do for themselves.

There are some effective, proactive strategies to use with children who vie for adult attention too often. One of the more successful is to redirect these children by assigning them a task. In completing a task that they perceive as important, these children can gain attention from others and be helpful at the same time. Another strategy is to plan times to spend with these children. You can purposefully engage these children in one-on-one conversation when they walk into the classroom first thing in the morning. This gives the child your attention before the child starts demanding it. You can also set up a special time for chats with these children, perhaps while walking to lunch or during a work activity time when other children are engaged individually or in small groups. A final strategy is to make a connection between the story the child wants to tell and the interests of another child then recommending that the child tell the story to another child who might be interested.

Supportive Language for Children Who Constantly Vie for Adult Attention

★ "I care about you and will spend time with you later _____ (at recess, after school, during writers' workshop, or some other appropriate time)."

★ "I know you like to spend time with just me. I would love to stay here with you, but right now I have to _____. Let's talk when _____."

★ "I know you want to tell me your story, but I have to listen to other children right now. If you will write about this today during writing time, I will read it."

★ "I would love to talk with you, but I can't at the moment. It is time for us to _____ (read a story, do our math, or whatever is next on the daily schedule)."

★ "Can you help me by checking the writing-center materials? I think there are some baskets that need filling."

★ (When they first come into the classroom in the morning) "I am so glad to see you. Today I want to listen to you read. Would you rather do that now or during DEAR time? Okay, then look for a book you would like to share with me."

STORY FROM A TEACHER

Ms. Susan Collins, 1st grade

From the moment Holly walked into the classroom, I felt like she was attached to my leg. She constantly wanted to be near me, to be touching me, and especially, to be talking to me. She was the youngest child of three, and the other

Continued next page

two children were major behavior problems. At home, they got all their parents' attention, not necessarily in a positive way, but Holly was virtually ignored. She was a compliant child, at home and in the classroom, except for always needing my attention. I think if I had let her, she would have had daylong conversations with me. I felt sorry for this little girl, but I could not let her consume all of my time. I had a class full of children who needed my attention as well. I tried giving her attention first thing in the morning before she started demanding my attention. I tried to find things for her to do in the classroom, so she felt like she was doing things to help me out, without being right next to me all the time. I tried to involve her with engaging activities with other children. I set up some signals that only we used, for "checking in" from time to time. Sometimes I just had to ignore her. It took weeks and weeks of being consistent with her, but over time, her behavior did change and she became less dependent on me.

CHILDREN WITH OTHER CHALLENGING BEHAVIORS

Beyond being physically aggressive, trying to boss other people, and constantly vying for adult attention, there are many other behaviors that can be challenging to the teacher, the other children in the class, even to the child exhibiting the behavior. Whatever the challenging behavior, there are five general strategies to use with these children:

1. Modeling — demonstrate the appropriate behavior or have other children in the class model it

2. Rehearsing appropriate behavior — provide opportunities for the child to practice the behavior

3. Role-playing — create situations for the child to practice the behavior in a context in which the behavior might be needed

4. Continuous reinforcement — provide reinforcement as the child practices the desired behavior

5. Prompting children — give children cues to help them remember how and when to use the new behavior

Supportive Language for Children Who Exhibit Other Challenging Behaviors

★ (First thing in the morning) "I know you are going to have a good day. Today you are going to use your self-control, right?"

★ "People are not for _____ (hitting, pushing, bullying, calling names, etc.), just like you are not for _____."

★ "I remember that you decided to _____. Thank you for practicing that just now."

★ "We are on our way to the _____ (restroom, lockers, etc.). Think in your brain about how that looks. Okay, now do it."

STORY FROM A TEACHER

Ms. Katherine Sheffield, kindergarten

David drove us all crazy—from me and his classmates to the principal, office staff, custodians, and cafeteria workers. David was a whiner. It didn't matter to whom he was talking or what he was talking about, his voice always had this twangy, whiney quality to it. It would get worse when he was upset, but that whine was constant. I tried lots of different things to try to get him to use a more normal voice. I modeled using a whiney voice and then a normal voice, trying to get him to hear the difference. I got other students to do that. I tried using puppets and role-play situations. The whiney voice continued, bothering other children to the point that they began excluding him from almost all of their activities. Finally, it came to me. Maybe David could hear the difference in our tones of voice but could not hear that in his own voice. With David's mother's agreement, I started audiotaping him at his whiniest. That seemed to do the trick. Finally, he could hear the difference between his whiney voice and his "normal" voice. Even after that, it took weeks for David to leave that whiney voice behind. He and I had lots of practice, role-playing, reminders, and cues. David wasn't a behavior problem in the regular sense of behavior problems, but that whiney voice was a challenging behavior for me.

Behavior Related to Inadequate Social Development

Children who exhibit challenging behaviors are not the only ones who may have difficulty becoming a part of the class community. Children whose social development is not age-appropriate may also have this problem. Some of these children lack the social skills necessary to interact successfully with their peers. Others may make decisions to withdraw from group situations. Both need as much support as children who exhibit challenging behaviors. Children with limited social skills need an adult to teach them appropriate skills and to encourage them in their efforts toward becoming more socially competent.

CHILDREN WHO LACK APPROPRIATE SOCIAL SKILLS TO INTERACT WITH PEERS

Some children enter early childhood classrooms prepared to work with other children; others do not. Whether the assignment is to work with a partner or in a group of three to six children, inevitably the same child (or children) is not selected as a partner or is

Positive TEACHER TALK

Supportive Language for Children Who Lack Appropriate Social Skills to Interact With Peers

★ "If you want to play grocery store with the others in the dramatic-play center, try walking up to them calmly and saying in a normal voice, 'Could I be a customer in your store?'"

★ (At the beginning of recess) "If you want to play soccer and other children have already started a game, you could say nicely, 'Could I play with you guys?' Try saying that."

★ "You seem to be feeling awkward. Tell me what you would like to do, and I will help you find the words to say to get that done."

★ "Other children do not know what you want unless you tell them. Let's figure out the words to tell them what you want."

told that some children do not want him or her in their group. When this happens, you can use some of the phrases offered in Chapter 5 in the discussion about helping children join an ongoing group (page 90). You can also work in ways that go beyond trying to support the rejected children. Identify potential partners for them (perhaps children who have similar interests or children who are particularly empathetic) and bring these children together in nonthreatening situations. For example, a socially competent child could be paired with a child who is often rejected to work together to prepare class snacks, to put together reclosable bags of math manipulatives for a class math game, or to take inventory of writing-center supplies. In each case, the more socially competent child models appropriate social skills as they work, and perhaps that child may discover a more likable side of the socially awkward child.

Beyond using socially competent children as models for more awkward children, social skills can be explicitly taught. To avoid singling out a child or a few children, teach these skills to the entire class.

CHILDREN WHO WITHDRAW FROM THE GROUP

Some children enter early childhood classes never having been part of a group of children before, and they honestly do not know how to get along with peers. They tend to be onlookers, hanging back, observing other children. Other children who withdraw from the group have developed a sense of inadequacy (Nelsen et al., 2000). They have given up on themselves and usually want to be left alone. For these children, it helps to break down a task into very small steps so they feel a sense of accomplishment as they work.

Positive TEACHER TALK

Supportive Language for Children Who Withdraw From the Group

★ "I see that you have chosen not to work with everyone. Right now you are choosing to work alone."

★ "I see that you have chosen to work alone. Would you be okay with working with one other person?"

★ "I would love it if you would sit beside me today during our class meeting."

★ (To another child in the class) "Jackie, Rose isn't sure she wants to sit with us during story time. Would you be willing to ask her to sit with you to listen to *Jump, Frog, Jump* when I read that story this morning?"

Anytime you can set up opportunities for success, you should. Encourage any positive attempts on the part of these children.

Some of the Children, Some of the Time

So far, this chapter has discussed children whose conduct and actions are at the opposite ends of the continuum—those with a range of challenging behaviors and those who withdraw from peers and sometimes, even adults. Whereas these children's behaviors are easy for adult observers to recognize, and we know without a doubt that they require our attention and support, all children in our classes may from time to time exhibit behaviors that indicate they need our support.

Even children who are typically socially competent and compliant have days when their behavior is atypical. A child who is normally pleasant and kind to her classmates may come into class one morning in a bad mood. Instead of joining her friends already engaged in an activity, she may find a private place in the room and rebuff anyone who approaches her. On the other hand, that bad mood may play out in a totally different way. She may push her way into a group of classmates, snatch what she wants from another child, and demand that everyone do things her way. Behavior this out of character signals something is not right, but you may not have a clue about what is causing this uncommon behavior.

Any number of occurrences cause withdrawal or aggressive behavior in some of our students some of the time. Perhaps the child is in the early stages of an ear infection or some other childhood disease. Even small changes in a child's life—such as a parent being out of town for a business trip, a new after-school child-care provider, or a sibling not feeling well—can cause a child's behavior to change. At other times, these uncharacteristic behaviors can be caused by rather large changes in the child's life. Events, such as separation or divorce of the child's parents, a death in the family, even a move into a new house, can trigger behaviors that are not typical.

Any child can have an off day; however, if atypical behaviors continue for more than a day or two, you need to talk with the child's family. Knowing what is happening in a child's life outside of school helps you know how best to support a child for whom aggressive or withdrawing behaviors are uncommon.

Whether we know the reason for a child's inappropriate behaviors or not, many of the strategies discussed in this chapter help us deal with them. Active listening, asking open-ended questions to encourage the child to talk about how he or she feels, reflecting their statements, and describing how we think they may be feeling are all strategies to support children in their times of need.

Just as we teach appropriate behaviors to our students, frequently we need to teach young children how to behave when they feel out of sorts. In these situations we might suggest activities that might help them feel a bit better: drawing a picture, listening to calming music, working with a special friend, doing an important task for an adult, etc. Generally, in these situations, the child simply needs an affirmation that he or she is valued and important.

So, remember that it is not uncommon for some of the children to need special attention for some of the time. As is true of everything that goes on in the classroom, our teacher talk sets the tone for how children deal with these problems. Using the suggested strategies and techniques supports your efforts to support the children.

Summary

Whatever the factors that contribute to the development of challenging behaviors in young children, you need to recognize that these children have needs that must be met before they can successfully change their negative behaviors. You need to explicitly teach appropriate behaviors, have children practice them, and reinforce the more positive behaviors.

Prologue

This book has discussed how important the language that we use with young children really is. Specific words and your tone of voice can dramatically affect children, for better or worse. Different chapters offered specific language that you can incorporate into your interactions with young children that will positively affect children's development.

Just as with any change in your life, it is best to begin small and set short-term goals that can be reached easily. For example, you might choose arrival time as a first priority. During arrival time, you can focus on language that helps set the tone for the day, in greeting each child individually, letting the child know that you are glad to see him or her, that you are interested in activities outside of school, and that you expect good things from him or her at school today. Or you might decide to drop the phrase "good job" from your interactions with children and try to use more meaningful, specific comments in responding to their work. Either one of these changes will require a certain amount of time. Simply making the decision to change a particular behavior does not mean that the change will occur without working on it. You will need to think of ways to remind yourself about this decision. You might leave yourself a note near the class door to remind yourself about the language change you are trying to make, wear a ring on a finger you don't normally wear jewelry, post a picture or photograph that triggers your memory, or simply tie a string around your wrist. You might even jot down specific phrases or sentences that you want to incorporate into your language with children on an index card and have the card nearby to serve as a resource. Other strategies you have used to support a personal change can be used to help you make the changes you want in your "teacher talk."

We wish you luck in making the changes you've identified as ones that will make you a better teacher.

Final Thoughts From Deborah

I started my teaching career as a 12-year-old, baby-sitting the neighbors' grand-children. But it was not until I was in my late 30s (and had several years of teaching experience) that it ever occurred to me to *think* about the words that I used with children.

My *aha* moment came as Deb Gist, a third-grade teacher, and I chatted while super-vising our students on the playground. As I noticed one of Deb's students heading toward us, she muttered something to the effect of, "Not again." But as Tara presented her case about "other girls being mean to me," Deb knelt beside her and focused her full attention on Tara. She looked into her eyes, listened to everything she had to say, then took a deep breath and sincerely commented, "It must have hurt when they said those things. Is this something you want to put on the agenda for our next class meeting?" Tara responded, "No, I don't think so," and walked away.

I asked Deb about her, and she explained that Tara constantly tried to get revenge on classmates who didn't treat her the way she wanted to be treated. At the beginning of the year, Tara wanted to use every class meeting as a forum to elaborate about how other children mistreated her. But over time, because Deb supported children in work-ing through their own problems, Tara was complaining less about others and trying to work out her own problems more often.

From that moment on, I purposefully listened to the way Deb interacted with children. I noted the words she said to them, how seriously she took their comments, and in turn, how children responded to her. As I adopted some of her language in my own class, the phrase that made the most difference that year was, "I will help you with your self-control." Rather than punishing a child for inappropriate behavior and saying, "Because you threw blocks, you cannot be in the block center anymore today," I positioned myself as a partner with the child in learning how to be self-controlled. The child still had to leave the block center, but that small difference in my language made a big difference in my interactions with children that year.

As I paid more attention to the language I used with children, I realized that my choice of "teacher talk" affected children deeply. I encourage you to step back and listen to yourself. Try to envision yourself as receiving a comment you make. Are there phrases you use that could unintentionally hurt children? Could you adapt phrases from this book to be more effective than the language you currently use? It takes time to change our day-to-day language, but Charlotte and I believe this is an important part of both helping children and being the most effective teacher you can be.

Final Thoughts From Charlotte

Charlotte Zolotow's poem "People" begins: "Some people talk and talk and never say a thing . . ." For me, she has captured the essence of talking to children—being succinct while challenging their thoughts to new levels.

My friend Katie distinguishes between the ways she talks to young children. When she directs or disciplines them, she uses what she calls the "German-shepherd method." It uses an economy of words, using "come," "go," "sit," and "stay" to give clear directions and communications. Young children's brains are not cluttered with, "Okay, guys. After we finish this, what I want you to start to do next is come to the circle." She simply begins with "Come to the circle." They immediately hear what they should do and quickly respond without processing through the unnecessary words or all that "talk and talk." But when Katie is engaging children in what she calls "accountable talk" she is much more probing and reflective. Here she draws out children's responses, using phrases like, "Tell me more" or "I'm not clear on that—can you explain it to me again?" when she really wants the child to clarify his or her own thoughts and think more deeply about them.

I think this is what *Positive Teacher Talk* is really about. It is learning to vary the ways you talk with children, while being consistent within those variations. For example, when a teacher sets a protocol for her response to a playground tiff, that response must be consistent. But when she is talking about the deeper meaning of a literature selection, she uses a different protocol. Different situations call for different "talk."

Our society increasingly celebrates activities that promote isolation. Think about vehicles decked out with DVD players, children sitting in restaurants watching a movie on their portable DVD player while the parents stare mindlessly at the big-screen plasma TV on the wall, and the ever-increasing popularity of video games. These are all solitary activities, with little need for enjoyment of communication. When Deborah and I were working on this book, we met at a local bookstore/coffee shop. While there, we noticed two college-age students who were apparently studying together. But both focused on their own laptop and each had earbuds from their individual MP3 players in their ears. Why did they bother to dress and drive there to meet together? As we watched, there was almost no communication until they were ready to leave. Then they simply stood up, said good-bye, and left.

Where will our children learn to communicate if not by our example as teachers? It is important to note that Zolotow's poem ends with, "Some people touch your hand and music fills the sky." That "music"—or the unlocking of the wonders of the world—is what we want for our children. Happy talking!

References

Bickart, Toni S., Judy R. Jablon, and Diane Trister Dodge. *Building the Primary Classroom: The Complete Guide to Teaching and Learning*. Washington, D.C.: Teaching Strategies, 1999.

Cameron, Caren, Colleen Politano, Daphne Macnaughton, and Betty Tate. *Recognition Without Rewards: Building Connections*. Winnipeg, MB, Canada: Portage & Main, 1997.

Charney, Ruth. *Teaching Children to Care: Classroom Management for Ethical and Academic Growth*. Turners Falls, MA: Northeast Foundation for Children, 1992.

Dalton, Joan, and Marilyn Watson. *Among Friends: Classrooms Where Caring and Learning Prevail*. Oakland, CA: Developmental Studies Center, 1997.

Denton, Paula, and Roxann Kriete. *The First Six Weeks of School*. Minneapolis, MN: Educational Media Corporation, 2000.

DeVries, Rheta, and Betty Zan. *Moral Classrooms, Moral Children: Creating a Constructivist Atmosphere in Early Childhood Education*. New York: Teachers College Press, 1994.

Diffily, Deborah, and Charlotte Sassman. *Project-Based Learning With Young Children*. Portsmouth, NH: Heinemann, 2002.

Flodin, Mickey. *Signing Illustrated*. New York: Perigee Trade, 1994.

Kaiser, Barbara, and Judy Sklar Rasminsky. *Challenging Behavior in Young Children: Understanding, Preventing, and Responding Effectively*. Boston: Allyn & Bacon, 2003.

Kohn, Alfie. *Beyond Discipline: From Compliance to Community*. Alexandria, VA: Association for Supervision and Development, 1996.

Kohn, Alfie. "Five Reasons to Stop Saying 'Good Job!'" *Young Children*, September 2001.

Kriete, Roxann. *The Morning Meeting Book*. Turners Falls, MA: Northeast Foundation for Children, 1999.

Nelsen, Jane, Lynn Lott, and H. Stephen Glenn. *Positive Discipline in the Classroom: Developing Mutual Respect, Cooperation, and Respect in Your Classroom*. New York: Three Rivers Press, 2000.

Perlmutter, Jane, and Louise Burrell. *The First Weeks of School: Laying a Quality Foundation*. Portsmouth, NH: Heinemann, 2001.

Rutter, Michael, Henri Giller, and Ann Hagell. *Antisocial Behavior by Young People*. Cambridge: Cambridge University Press, 2000.

Notes